Three Bodies

Three Bodies

Reiley Wieland

**Cover Art by Nick Evans,
To the Moon Studios**

Short & Sweet Publishing
ISBN: 978-1-7375667-3-1

From the Author

Usually, I try to write a long, beautiful dedication to all the people that have supported me while I wrote the book. However, this book was HARD! Crime novels are very involved! It was like making a puzzle in my mind, then dismantling the pieces, mixing 'em all up, and then expecting someone else to see the picture. And did I mention my dog, Dira, ate a few of the pieces? My brain is exhausted, so I'm gonna keep this Short & Sweet!

Thanks to the women that support me—you know who you are. If you aren't sure, go ahead and give yourself a pat on the back just in case.

Thanks to Rheanna M—you sent the meme that sparked an idea that turned into a novel.

My Favorite Murder—the podcast that fosters my love of true crime and gave me plenty of ideas for the perfect crime. SSDGM

About the Author

I live in a small town in central Nebraska. My constant companion is my dog, Dira, a 3-year-old rescue. She is a super sweet cuddle bug that I love dearly—even if she gets a little gassy sometime. Sweet Pea, my 27-year-old Mustang mare, is also alive and kicking and enjoying her retirement. When I'm not writing, I do anything that keeps my hands busy: wood working, refurbishing furniture, making wall décor, string art….and the list goes on.

As a side note, I am not a very good cook. Occasionally I can make a meal that isn't burnt, but that's the exception, not the rule. Therefore, the recipes used in this book are pieced together with research. I have tried most of them and they are pretty tasty, but don't put all your culinary dreams on my shoulders.

This is my fourth publication. If you like this book, you may enjoy my debut novel, *After the Final Curtain*, a story about strong women facing adversity. Or, if you have any youngsters that like animals, check out my children's chapter books *The Adventures at the Short & Sweet Ranch*, under my pen name, Nadine Davies.

Chapter 1
Grace Whitmore

Tonight's the night, Grace. Tonight's the night.

I repeated those words over and over in my head as I waited in line to get into the cowboy bar, Barn Sour. I've become a regular here since it no longer takes three buses to get to the outskirts of Omaha from the city center where I live. My new job as a receptionist at the hospital pays me enough to afford to take a cab and come more often. Ultimately, this increases my chances of finally meeting the man of my dreams, of meeting my country boy. And tonight, is that night!

A country boy isn't quite the same as a Southern gentleman. Growing up in Georgia, I was courted by many Southern gentlemen who had been taught proper manners and how to treat a lady. These country boys are rougher around the edges but aren't bad men. Who better to smooth out those edges than a young lady named Grace?

"ID," the bouncer asked gruffly when I reached the front of the line.

I handed it over, and he studied it closely. I flashed him my best smile. Between that and my big, blonde hair, there was no mistaking that I was the one in the photo. But I got this reaction anytime someone from Nebraska saw my Georgia driver's license.

"It's real, sugar," I said in my Southern drawl. "Now, can I go dance my Southern peach off?"

He laughed heartily and waved me through the door.

There was a crowd three deep at the bar, but I managed to push my way to the front and climb onto a stool. I waited for Jason, the bartender, to finish popping the tops off the beers lined up on the bar before I flagged him down.

He nodded at me, and I relaxed on the stool. My toe was already tapping to the beat of the music. Jason set a glass of orange-and-pink liquid in front of me a minute later.

"Fuzzy navel, Miss Grace," Jason said.

"Jason, I've told you just to call me Grace." I took a sip of the drink. "It's delicious as always."

"I've been practicing just for you," he said with a wink.

"Can you hide my purse again?"

He took my purse and tucked it under the bar. "Is he here tonight?"

"Why do you think I'm wearing my lucky purple boots?" I asked, lifting my foot so he could see the purple leather boots. "He's here for sure. Wish me luck! And when I come up for the next round, I want to hear about that writing course you've been taking. I want the first copy of your novel."

"You got it," he said.

I jumped off the barstool and pushed through the crowd into the main area of the dance hall. The bar is on one side of the big, square room, just inside the entrance. Opposite, a local band was already on the stage, cranking out some classic country music hits. The other two sides were filled with booths, tables, and chairs. The sunken, wood dance floor was in the middle. It was already filled with dancers, some solos, and some couples.

I took my seat at a table close to the dance floor. I like to enjoy my drink and watch the crowd to scout any potential men I want to dance with. After all, the *he* Jason was referring to was the man I hoped to have an instant connection with. If he was here, he would surely be on that dance floor. After emptying my glass, I ate the orange slice and bounced out of my seat. I was ready to hit the dance floor!

I slid into an open space in the crowd. Women in low-cut jeans and flannel shirts knotted under their bosoms surrounded me. I was wearing a floral summer dress that flared with every turn. I laughed and cheered with the crowd, not embarrassed or self-conscious. I felt myself come alive!

I danced through "Boot Scootin' Boogie," "Watermelon Crawl," and "Achy Breaky Heart" before I noticed the stranger dressed in black dancing beside me. He didn't say anything but smiled at me every time I twirled. He had the most beautiful smile, with straight white teeth and adorable dimples. The man's jaw was so sharp it could cut glass. But it was those dark, soulful eyes that made me trip on my own feet.

I fell in slow motion, like a scene from a romantic comedy. Without missing

2

a step, the stranger wrapped his arms around me, catching me. Everyone disappeared, and all I could see was him. Maybe it was because his face was so close to mine. Or perhaps it was because his felt cowboy hat blocked everything out. It didn't matter, though. The only thing I was certain of was that he was the only person in the room that mattered.

"Don't worry, I've got you," he whispered.

All I could do was gulp.

"Take a breath," he said gently.

I did.

"And let me buy you a drink."

I could only blink dumbly as he tilted me back onto my feet.

"What can I get you from the bar?" he asked.

"A nuzzy favel," I blurted. "I mean, a fuzzy navel."

He smiled. "One fuzzy navel coming up. Don't move."

I nodded, but as soon as he disappeared into the crowd, I made a beeline for the ladies' room. I'd already made a fool of myself during my first impression, so I needed to make a better second one. I had to make sure my hair and makeup were perfect. I quickly dabbed the sheen of sweat from my forehead and pinched some color into my cheeks. I smoothed my dress, then pulled a tube of lipstick from the hidden pocket. I reapplied it so my heart-shaped lips looked plump and perfect. Last, I flipped my head upside down and tossed my hair, volumizing my blonde curls.

I raced back onto the dance floor, skidding to a halt as he reappeared from the crowd. He was holding two drinks above his head and out of reach of the dancers. I took the fuzzy navel when he offered it, our fingers briefly touching. He motioned away from the dance floor, so I led him to my seat.

I glanced at the bar. Jason's head popped up above the crowd. His look of concern sent a shot of fear down my spine. He glanced at the man beside me, then held two fingers up to his eyes in the "I'm watching you" gesture. I gave him a thumbs-up, and he gave me a quick grin before disappearing behind the crowd.

"Looks like you've got a watchdog at the bar," the cowboy said.

"That's Jason. We've become friends, so he watches out for me."

"He's a good man, then," he said. "But I am, too, I promise."

"That sounds like something a bad man would say," I challenged. Then I remembered my manners. "My heavens, I just realized I haven't even introduced myself. I'm Grace. Grace Whitmore."

"That's a beautiful name, Miss Whitmore." He held his hand out to me. "My name's Cass."

I took his hand in mine. I was surprised by how smooth his hands were. I'd danced with enough cowboys to know their hands were usually dry and calloused. I liked this better, though.

"Tell me, Grace Whitmore, what is a beautiful lady like yourself doing in a dirty cowboy bar like this?"

I smiled at the compliment. "I like dancing. And I like the people. And the fuzzy navels."

"And you're hoping to find someone special," Cass guessed.

"Hopefully, if I'm lucky." I took another sip of my drink. "My daddy would prefer I move back home to Georgia and let him find me a suitable gentleman to marry."

"But you don't want that." It was a statement, not a question.

"No, I don't," I said. "I know my daddy is doing what he thinks is best, but I want to find someone when the timing is right. I want to tell my children and grandchildren the romantic story of how I met the love of my life."

"I had a feeling you were a romantic," he said.

"I'm hopelessly romantic!"

"You deserve to have that romantic story. I hope you get it."

I blushed, then turned the question back on him. "How about you? Why do you come to this dirty cowboy bar?"

"Because I'm a dirty cowboy," Cass said plainly. "Please, tell me more about you."

"What do you want to know?"

"Everything," he answered.

We spent the next hour dancing and talking. We jumped out of our seats and ran to the dance floor when we heard a song we loved. We two-stepped and line-danced until I was hot and my hair fell flat. When we grew tired, we would sit and fall effortlessly back into conversation. I told him everything about my life, from my first pony as a child to my new life in Omaha.

". . . . the hospital is fun for now, but it's not my dream," I finished.

"What's your dream?" he asked.

"It's stupid," I said sheepishly. "It'll never really happen."

"Miss Whitmore, there is no such thing as a stupid dream."

Cass said it with such sincerity that my heart swelled. I could tell that no matter what I told him, he would do everything possible to make my dreams

4

come true.

"I want to be a singer." Before he could speak, I rushed on. "I know it's what every girl says, but I do love singing."

"I think that's a great dream," Cass said.

"Really?"

"Yes, really." He smiled. "You would get to see the world when you go on tour."

"Honestly, I would be happy just singing the National Anthem at smaller events. You know, football games, fairs, rodeos. That sort of thing."

"Rodeos, huh?" His eyes lit up. "Miss Whitmore, I think tonight is your lucky night."

"Why is that?"

"Because I'm a saddle bronc rider," he explained. "I've been on the rodeo circuit a long time and have a good relationship with most of the promoters. They are the ones that hire all the talent, from the announcers to the livestock contractors."

"Do you mean you might be able to get me a job singing?" I jumped to my feet and put my hands on his shoulders, unable to contain my excitement.

"I can't promise anything, but I can put in a good word."

"Oh, my goodness, thank you, Cass!" I threw my arms around him and squeezed hard.

He hesitated a second, then reciprocated. He held me tight for a long time. His hands began moving slowly up and down my back, and I felt myself relax into his body. It took every ounce of self-control to push away from him. I smoothed my dress as I sat back down.

"All right, all right, enough about me," I chastised. "It's your turn. You must tell me something about yourself."

He spent the next few songs telling me about his life on the rodeo circuit. He had been riding in rodeos since he was barely able to walk. It never occurred to him to try anything else. He'd won plenty of buckles but hadn't qualified for any national titles. Yet.

"Until then, I'll keep driving from town to town, sleeping in cheap motel rooms and drinking in dirty cowboy bars."

"Don't you ever miss home, though?"

"Not really. My only family left is a brother back home," he said. "I stop by if I'm ever within 50 miles of his house, but that's not often."

"Doesn't he miss you?" I took his hand to show my concern.

"I'm sure he does a little." Cass paused for a moment as though in thought, then continued. "He's a cop, though, so he's got enough to worry about without thinking of my dangerous career. And he understands that rodeo is my life."

"I'm glad you have someone that supports you, at least." I gave his hand a reassuring squeeze.

"Yeah, I'm lucky to have that. The worst part of the rodeo life is all the cheap motels. I've stayed in some rooms that were probably murder crime scenes at some point."

"That's awful," I said, my nose wrinkled. "I'd get tired of eating at restaurants and gas stations. Nothing beats a good home-cooked meal."

"I don't actually eat out too much," he said.

I furrowed my brows. "How can that be with you being on the road?"

"I cook most of the time," he explained. "I've got a great setup in the back of my truck: grill, gas stove, utensils, everything. I've even got a cooler that plugs into my cigarette lighter so I can keep things cold."

"That's so impressive. What's your favorite thing to make?" I asked.

"I make a delicious chicken fried steak with all the fixings. Corn with bacon, mashed potatoes, country gravy, and peach cobbler for dessert. You'd probably like it."

"Stop teasing me," I drawled, slapping his arm playfully. "That's my favorite meal. But you'll be hard-pressed to beat my Mama's chicken fried steak."

"I'd be willing to try."

"But there's no way you can cook all that from the back of your truck. You must be bluffing."

"Cross my heart and hope to die." Cass drew an X over his heart. "Would you like to see it?"

He was so excited to show me something he was proud of that I immediately said yes.

"Let me just get my purse," I said.

Cass followed me through the crowd. I could feel his body close to mine, feel his heat burning me. At the bar, I waved down Jason. He handed me my purse, and his eyes flashed behind me to Cass.

"Is this him?" Jason whispered.

"I think it might be," I said, unable to stop smiling.

"What's his name?"

"Cass. Isn't it unique and wonderful?"

"Sure, let's go with that," he said skeptically. "Be careful, Miss Grace. Have fun but be careful."

"You've got it. I'll let you know how it goes." I turned back at the last second. "Don't think I've forgotten about that book. I want to know more next time I come in."

We slipped quickly out the door. Even though it was the middle of the night, the air was still hot and muggy. The slight breeze offered no relief because it was just blowing hot air around. August in Nebraska is the worst month.

We strolled through the parking lot, not hurrying to get to his truck. We enjoyed each other's company. At one point, a big, black Suburban flew through the parking lot, kicking up dust and gravel. Cass picked me up and whirled me out of danger, setting me gently back on my feet. I thought he would kiss me as he held me close, but he stepped back reluctantly.

When we reached the far side of the parking lot, he unlocked the doors of a small, dark-colored pickup truck with a hard top cover on the bed. He opened the top window and dropped the tailgate. Inside was a steel box that resembled an old magician's trunk. He began opening doors, pulling out drawers, and uncovering utensils. I could see an entire kitchen's worth of cookware.

"That's pretty impressive," I said, peering over everything. One drawer was full of sharp knives. "Is it safe to travel with these knives in here?"

"Sure, it is. The knives aren't so dangerous if you know how to use them." He leaned forward and grabbed something dark from the kit.

"This cast iron skillet is the real danger. It could break a toe if you dropped it. Or smash a skull."

I turned toward him. "Why would a skillet smash—"

Chapter 2

D etective, Detective!" The scream rang across the restaurant. "We
have an *emergency!*"

I instinctively reached for my holster, but it wasn't on my hip.
I didn't have my weapon because today I was supposed to be Dawson Falco,
proud husband to a loving wife, not Detective Falco of the Omaha Police
Department's Homicide Division. I searched the room for the usual signs of
an emergency but saw no running, screaming, or trampling. I only saw a tall,
thick man with overworked hair flouncing toward me. I sighed, knowing that
the screamer, Jean-Pierre, had a different definition of *emergency* than I did.

Jean-Pierre was exhausted when he reached me and had to lean against the
hostess stand for support. He held up a finger to signal me to wait. So, I waited.
I didn't have a choice. He was helping me throw a celebratory luncheon today.
He knew I couldn't pull it off without his *queer eye*—his words, not mine. And
I knew that *he* would crack under the pressure to be perfect if I wasn't careful.

Jean-Pierre was the *maître d'* at Clever Culinary, a contemporary restaurant
in Omaha that had been packed nearly every night since it opened almost three
years ago. He was the right-hand man to the head chef and owner, Harper.
Whether it was ordering supplies, hiring staff, or dealing with the rare unruly
customer, Jean-Pierre was there. He swore that no matter how good the food
was, the restaurant would not survive without him.

Harper agrees with him, too, though she would never tell him, fearing he
would stage a coup. She only tells me because I'm her husband. We married
only months before Clever Culinary opened. I've supported her dreams and
ambitions and tried to help her however possible, except in the kitchen. I've

been known to burn water, so I'm not allowed near a stove. Today, I was throwing this luncheon in Harper's honor.

As a detective for the Omaha Police Department in Omaha, Nebraska, I've orchestrated 30-person operations to stop drug cartels. I've gone under- cover in a sex trafficking ring. And I've worked security in the roughest area of Sturgis Bike Week. As intense and dangerous as all those situations were, they were nothing compared to the stress level I'd felt while organizing this luncheon. I want it to be perfect for Harper. Hence, Jean-Pierre's presence.

Finally, Jean-Pierre had caught his breath. "It's the napkins. They are wrong, *all wrong*! It's a *disaster*!"

"Jean-Pierre, what do you mean that they are wrong?"

"It's too horrible to say, but I will *persist*," he said dramatically, emphasizing too many words as usual. "I ordered the cloth napkins in *royal* purple, but they came in *plum* purple!"

He held up a napkin and a color swatch from Harper's book of linen options. They looked the same to me. I knew I had to play this just right, or Jean-Pierre would have a full-scale meltdown. I held them up to the light and pretended to scrutinize them.

"Jean-Pierre, I assure you, you are the only person with an eye keen enough to notice the difference." He didn't look convinced. "Even my trained eye for detail as a detective can't see the difference."

He eyed me skeptically. "I'm going to ask Detective Leoni. She's got the *woman's* touch on her side." He snatched the napkin and book out of my hands and bounded off.

I stared at him in disbelief, then continued through my checklist. The wait staff and I had been working all morning to rearrange the restaurant. We'd moved the tables into a U-shape to accommodate the twenty guests who RSVP'd for the celebration. I could hear Harper's sous chefs pre-paring the meal, and hors d'oeuvres were already being brought out and set on ice. So far, things were going surprisingly well, the napkin fiasco notwithstanding.

I checked my watch. It was 11:00, and guests would start showing up any minute now.

Another person rushed up to me. "The purple is wrong! The purple is wrong!"

It was Detective Sophia Leoni, my partner in the Homicide Division. She leaned against the hostess stand, throwing her arm dramatically over her face like a damsel in distress. I rolled my eyes, but I was glad to see her.

"Jean-Pierre found you, I assume."

"Yes, but I assured him that even my lady eyes can't see the difference in the purples."

"Crisis averted," I said.

"Where's Harper?" she asked.

"She should be here soon. She was still sleeping when I left this morning."

"I figured she'd be here trying to take over the kitchen?"

"Usually, she would be," I agreed. "She did a cooking competition in North Platte yesterday and didn't get home until early this morning. I convinced her to sleep in."

"Probably a good thing, too. Harper doesn't need to see this train wreck before it gets cleaned up." She elbowed me in the ribs.

I scoffed at her. "Would you please go do something helpful?"

"You aren't the boss of me," she said.

"I am your superior, though," I pointed out.

"You're an ass is what you are." She stuck her tongue out at me before heading off to be helpful.

Sophia wasn't wrong. I'm not her boss, just her partner. And I am her superior only because I started at the Omaha Police Department right out of the Police Academy. I grew up in Omaha and never wanted to live anywhere else.

Sophia is originally from Chicago. She was raised by her father, who was also a detective. After his death, she wanted a change of scenery. My last partner retired, so she transferred here a year ago. She wasn't a large or intimidating woman, but I had seen her square up with criminals and chauvinists twice her size. However, Sophia wasn't here today as my partner but as Harper's friend. The first time I introduced them, they bonded immediately over their love of teasing me.

The glass door to the restaurant swung open as the first guests arrived. Jean-Pierre ushered them toward the bar, where they were served drinks, then to the hors d'oeuvres buffet. I had taken great care to ensure everyone invited was a true friend to Harper. Most of the guests were friends or mentors from the restaurant industry.

At 11:30, Harper arrived, wearing a flowy sundress that accentuated her thin torso and long legs. Her hair was an adorable messy pixie cut, and she had pinned a big daisy above her ear. Her big eyes sparkled with excitement when she saw all her guests. And her smile—boy, did I love her smile—was radiant! I ran to her and enveloped her in a bear hug, spinning her around.

"What's all this?" Harper asked through a laugh.

"It's your celebration luncheon, of course." I set her down.

"I thought we were just having a quiet lunch with a few people?"

"Harper, you deserve to be admired and celebrated." Then I whispered, "Don't worry, I had Sophia double-check the guest list."

"You are a smart man," she teased.

I showed her to the bar. She waved at people as we walked. Once she had a drink in her hand, she said, "You know me so well, honey. I like everyone here. Especially you."

I winked at her. From the corner of my eye, I saw Jean-Pierre coming toward us. I quickly whispered to Harper, "Whatever you do, tell Jean-Pierre that the purple is perfect."

"Harper, darling, you are *gorgeous*," Jean-Pierre twittered. "Tell me, *what* do you think of the decorations?"

"Everything is beautiful, Jean-Pierre," she replied, kissing him on both cheeks. "The purple is perfect."

Jean-Pierre beamed. "I knew you'd love it! I didn't dare let your *delicious caveman* of a husband make any decisions about the décor, or it would've all been *mauve*." He covered his mouth in horror.

"We wouldn't want that, would we," Harper said.

"Let's not be *too* hard on him, darling; he did plan this *wonderful* party for you. He couldn't have pulled it off without *me*, of course." He winked at me. "Has he shown you his other *spectacular* gift yet? It truly is *divine!*"

He pulled her off the bar stool and showed her to my other surprise: her wall of fame. Harper was so modest about her achievements that she felt embarrassed to show them off. So, I did it for her. I had taken all her awards, magazine articles, and cover pages to a professional to have them matted and framed. Then I'd given the frames to Jean-Pierre to arrange on the wall. It was a spectacular display of her achievements.

She beamed with pride when she saw her hard work on display. She covered her eyes when she saw her picture from the cover of *Top Chef* magazine. Her hair was done up in a tall pouf. It was fashionable in 2016. In 2022, it's just embarrassing. The guests surrounded her, asking about the photoshoots and if she'd met any celebrity chefs. I retreated so she could enjoy the spotlight.

I caught my reflection in the restaurant's front window. I may not be the most handsome man in Omaha, but I wouldn't describe myself as a *caveman*. I was over six feet tall, and I had broad shoulders and a barrel chest like a professional wrestler. My dark hair was long enough to tuck behind my ears, but I had cut off my ponytail before I married Harper. She was happy I did but forbade me from ever shaving my face. She liked my sexy stubble.

At precisely noon, Jean-Pierre clapped his gloved hands and directed everyone to their seats. Conversation flowed smoothly during appetizers and laughter erupted throughout the main meal. Harper enjoyed speaking with Alice, her baker friend who supplied the restaurant with fresh bread. After the staff cleared all the plates, I stood and clinked my spoon against my glass of scotch.

"Thank you, everyone, for joining me today to celebrate another one of Harper's accomplishments."

The group clapped. Harper raised her glass in thanks.

"In the five years since I met Harper, there have been many contests, many interviews, and many wins. And I'm proud of her every time she reaches another goal. Only once have I ever been happy that she lost. And that was on the day we met.

"For those who don't know our origin story, we met at a chicken wing cook-off. Harper's wings were delicious, the perfect blend of spicy and sweet." I did a chef's kiss for emphasis.

"Fortunately, Harper got beat by some idiot who used a store-bought sauce! Even *I* knew that was basically cheating. Of course, I marched up to her and told her I thought she should've won. She flashed me that beautiful smile and said, "I know." The next thing I knew, I was helping her load her equipment into her truck, and she had asked me on a date."

The crowd laughed quietly.

"In the five years since then, she's been Nebraska's Top Chef and Omaha's youngest 5-Star rated chef. She even made it to the final round of *Cooked*, but those judges were idiots for not choosing her as the winner." The guests shouted their agreement. "But now, she's won her biggest prize yet! Everyone, please, raise a toast for the 2022 Midwestern States Chef of the Year!"

Everyone clapped and cheered. Sophia let out a piercing wolf-whistle.

Harper pulled me down for a kiss. When the applause settled down, I continued.

"Before I forget, Harper is also working on the final touches of her first cookbook. It'll be out in time for Christmas, and she's already sold almost 500 copies on preorder! If you want a signed copy, please talk to Jean-Pierre to order. Harper, tell us more about the cookbook."

Harper stood, uneasy at the idea of promoting herself. "As Dawson said, this is my first cookbook. I've finally decided on a title: *Travel on a Full Stomach: An Around-the-World Journey of Food and Friends*. It's full of recipes I learned while I traveled Europe, Asia, and Australia, among other places. They are all beginner recipes, so all of you can try them. Or you can come here to Clever Culinary, and I'll make them for you.

"Thank you all for coming today to celebrate with me. Having you all here means a lot to me. And thanks to Jean-Pierre and Dawson for organizing everything. Though I appreciate all the hard work you put into my wall of fame, as you called it, I have some bad news." She gave me a dramatic frown. "You'll have to make room for one more award because you are all looking at the 2022 Pork Belly Cook-Off Champion!"

Everyone raised their glasses again and cheered. I stood beside Harper and kissed her. When the applause died, I nodded to Jean-Pierre to bring dessert. He pushed through the swinging door to the kitchen to line up the servers.

Before the desserts emerged through the door, my cell phone rang. *The Imperial March* caught several guests' attention, including Sophia. It was the ringtone assigned to our boss, Chief Probst. And it always meant bad news.

"I'll be right back, Harper."

I caught Sophia's eye and nodded at her to follow me. We left the restaurant and stood in the overwhelming heat of August in Nebraska.

I answered the phone and put it on speaker mode. "Chief, you've got Falco and Leoni here."

"We've got a new case," Chief Probst barked. "Get down to Barn Sour."

"What's Barn Sour?" I asked, though I could see Sophia already googling it.

"It's a cowboy bar on the West side," he grunted. "We've got a dead girl behind a dumpster."

"Shit. We'll be there as soon as we can." I looked through the restaurant's window and saw Harper talking to Jean-Pierre. I turned to Sophia. "She's going to be mad."

"No, she won't, she'll understand," she said. "Harper supports your job, just like you support hers."

When we got back inside, Harper stood up and hugged Sophia. "I know you have to go," she said.

"Yeah, duty calls," Sophia said. She turned to me. "Dawson, I'll take my car and meet you there. I'd hate to scare you with my crazy driving."

"I appreciate that," I said with a laugh.

After Sophia left, Harper turned to me. "Stay safe; get the bad guy," she said as she always did when I left for a new case.

I gave her a kiss that was too long to be appropriate in front of the guests. "I'm sorry we have to leave before dessert," I whispered in her ear. "Enjoy the rest of your party. I love you."

She hugged me tight. "Don't worry, you'll get your dessert," she nipped my ear the way she knows drives me wild. "Several helpings of dessert."

Travel on a Full Stomach: An Around-the-World Journey of Food and Friends

Dear Chefs, Cooks, Bakers, and Readers,

For ten years, in my 20s and 30s, I traveled the world learning everything I could about the culinary arts. It started with a summer in Scotland, but I was so inspired that I had to keep going! I didn't want to be pegged down to one type of cooking. And in a time where all recipes are being updated, elevated, or deconstructed, I want to honor the cultures they came from. From Paris to Mexico, desserts to wild game, and ancient to modern, I have tried to include as many cultures and nationalities as possible.

Of course, I didn't do all this learning alone. I met so many amazing people along the way. I worked with some of the best chefs in the best restaurants in the world. I became friends with restaurant patrons, locals, and others connected to the food industry. I could not have done it without them. This cookbook is to show appreciation to them all.

Other people deserve my gratitude that came into my life after my travels: My editor, Dira D, and my publishing house, Short & Sweet Publishing; my sous chef and staff at my restaurant, Clever Culinary, in Omaha, NE; and my friends that always give me their honest opinions about my food. Last but certainly not least, my husband, Dawson Falco. I can't wait for a lifetime of cooking with you.

Your Friend,

Chef Harper

Chapter 3

Barn Sour was set on top of a small hill off Highway 275. Despite my GPS, I would've missed it if it weren't for the lines of police cars by the road. I pulled in and found an empty parking spot behind Sophia. A glance at the temperature gauge on my dashboard showed 98°. A nice cool day in August.

I saw her standing by the dumpster that Chief Probst had mentioned. She disappeared every time a white-suited lab technician walked in front of her. It's one of the curses of only being five feet tall, so she tells me. She'd tied her long, black hair in a ponytail, but the little flyaways were already stuck to her olive skin with sweat.

"What do we have, Sophia?"

"Dead woman. Twenty-two years old." She was looking at a sealed, clear evidence bag. "Found by the bar's manager when he took out the trash an hour ago. There's no sign of sexual assault, and her wallet and purse don't appear to be missing anything. That means this probably wasn't a robbery. The techs just found her ID."

She handed me the evidence bag. A Georgia driver's license with a blood smear revealed the woman as Grace Whitmore.

"Do we have a cause of death?" I asked.

"Yeah, this one's pretty obvious," she said. "Take a look."

We stepped closer to the dumpster and were enveloped by the stench. The victim was lying in the gravel, tucked partially behind the dumpster, in an apparent attempt to hide the body. She was petite, only a few inches taller than Sophia. Her hair was blonde except where it was matted with blood and dirt. She was pretty, too. Or, she had been until the blunt force trauma to her temple had taken it away.

"Ouch," I whispered. "Do we have a weapon?"

"I think I just found it!" a voice called from inside the dumpster.

A person wearing full safety gear popped up. She pulled down her mask and removed her goggles, and I realized it was Cathy, the County Coroner. Though it was below her pay grade to dumpster dive, Cathy enjoyed escaping the morgue and getting her hands dirty. She mostly enjoys sharing her dark sense of humor with the living, as opposed to her usual deceased audience.

Cathy was panting hard from the effort of rummaging through the trash. But she smiled when she held up her prize, a large black object now safely secured in an evidence bag.

"What is that?" Sophia asked.

"A cast iron skillet," Cathy replied. "Just like my grandma uses."

I took the bag from her. Dried blood the color of rust coated half the pan, and several of our victim's blonde hairs were visible. As a formality, Cathy's team would run all the appropriate tests at the lab for when the case went to trial, but the skillet was definitely our murder weapon.

"Does the bar serve food?" I asked.

"No," Sophia answered, "Just beer and liquor."

"And bad choices," Cathy added.

I chuckled. "You're probably not wrong, Cathy. But what would a cast iron skillet be doing in the dumpster of a bar that doesn't cook food?"

"Cowboys," Cathy said, leaning casually against the edge of the dumpster. When Sophia and I looked at her blankly, she rolled her eyes. "Come on, Falco. You're a Nebraska boy. Leoni's from Chicago, so she gets a pass, but you should know this."

"What do I know about cowboys?" I challenged. "I was born and raised in Omaha. The only time I've been around real cowboys was when Harper and I accidentally went to Vegas during National Finals Rodeo week."

"Falco, Falco, Falco," Cathy scolded, shaking her head. "You're a disappointment to every terrible country song about growing up in the Midwest."

"All right, all right, I get it." I threw my hands up, "I'm a disgrace. Could you please enlighten us on what cowboys have to do with our case? And get out of the dumpster, please. You look far too comfortable in there."

We helped Cathy down, and she removed the rest of her protective gear. We all moved from the area, so her team could finish processing the body and load it into the coroner's van.

17

"Cathy, you were saying?" I pushed.

"Right, as I was saying." Cathy wiped the sweat from her brow with her sleeve. "Professional cowboys travel the rodeo circuits across the US every year. Omaha is a central hub for a bunch of the big rodeos around Chicago, Kansas City, and Denver. Cowboys often stop here to rest, maybe hit up a few local rodeos for practice, and then move on. Of course, while they're here, they want to visit the only cowboy bar in 200 miles."

"Ok, that all makes sense," Sophia said, "But where does the frying pan come in?"

"Since the cowboys are on the road eight months a year, and most of them live off their last cash prize, they look for ways to save money—"

"I would think staying away from bars would be a good start," I interjected.

"Well, *obviously*, Falco," Cathy said sarcastically, "But cowboys count hops and barley toward their daily veggie intake. May I continue?"

"Please," I said, suppressing a laugh.

"To save money, some cowboys cook their own meals on kitchen kits in their trucks."

My brain finally caught up to Cathy's train of thought. "Ok, I know what you're talking about. Harper has a fancy toolbox kit that she uses when she does the cooking competitions," I said. "Hers is a professional setup, but I've seen really simple ones, too."

"And I'm sure she's always telling you it's cheaper to cook at home than eat fast food all the time," Sophia pointed out.

"Curious," Cathy added, "A chef with a popular restaurant saying not to eat out?"

"She only tells me that so I don't spoil my appetite by going to Burger King," I said in Harper's defense.

"If I were married to your wife, I would never eat anything other than her cooking," Cathy said.

"I'll tell Harper you said that."

"No need, Falco," Cathy patted me patronizingly on the shoulder, "Harper already knows I love her cooking. She also knows she could trade you for me whenever she wants."

"*Anyway*," Sophia said, trying to get the conversation back on track.

"What kitchen stuff is in these kits?"

"Anything and everything, depending on what they are cooking," I said. "Pots, pans, bowls, knives. They usually have a small gas grill or a camping stove, too."

"What are the chances we'll be able to pull a usable fingerprint off the skillet?" Sophia asked.

"Highly unlikely," Cathy said. "The surface is too bumpy to get a solid print."

"Thanks, Cathy," I nodded to her, then turned to Sophia. "Let's go chat with the guy that found the body."

"That would be the manager," she told me, leading me toward the bar. "He's waiting inside to talk to us. I'm going to let you handle this one. You are the boss, after all."

I rolled my eyes as we stepped onto the bar's wooden porch. The covered porch ran the whole length of the bar, like in an old Western movie. Inside the main door was a short, narrow hallway where the bouncer checked IDs. In the main bar area, the lights were all turned on, but the bar still seemed dark and dingy.

The manager, a man in his late thirties, sat at a table. He wore a typical cowboy outfit: black felt cowboy hat, plaid pearl-snap shirt, and tight jeans. His leather boots tapped the wooden floor as he feverishly bounced his leg under the table. We were within a few feet of him before he noticed us. I introduced myself and Sophia.

"Thank you for meeting with us, Mr.—" I started.

"Andrews. Andy Andrews," he said. "But call me Andy."

"Andy," I continued. "Could you tell us what happened this morning? Starting with the time you got to the bar."

"S-sure," Andy stammered. "I got here at about 11:00, like usual. We don't open until 5:00, but I do all the books and paperwork and finish the cleaning. I like the quiet before we open."

"No one else was here, then?"

"No, my bartender didn't come in until noon," he said. "At 12:30, I took the trash out."

"Can you describe what you saw?"

"I almost didn't see her," he whispered. "She was on the far side, so I almost missed her. But I saw the purple boots. My first thought was, *who would buy purple boots?* Then, *why would someone throw away a good pair of boots?* I grabbed them to throw them away but realized someone was still wearing them."

Andy burst into tears. I felt horrible for the guy. Cops, CSI techs, coroners—we're all so jaded from years on the job that we aren't bothered by death. Andy and other witnesses will probably never recover from their experience of finding a body. Sophia and I waited patiently until he was ready to continue.

"Have you ever seen the woman here before?" I asked quietly.

"Yeah, she came in pretty regularly," he said. "She's been coming in a few times a week for months. She's always polite to the staff and never causes problems. We all enjoy having her here."

"You seem to know a lot about her," I accused.

Andy's eyes widened in panic. "No, I didn't know her. Like, I didn't know her name or anything. But she mostly comes in alone. All my employees keep an eye on the singles to make sure they don't get into trouble."

"What kind of trouble are you expecting?" I asked.

"Just the usual bar problems: getting too drunk, fighting, men getting handsy," he explained.

"Does that happen a lot?"

"Not more than any other bar." Andy suddenly got defensive. "Look, I know every country song makes it sound like cowboys and country boys are perfect gentlemen, but they're still *men*. They still think rules don't apply to them and women belong to them just like any other adrenaline junkie alpha male." He leaned back and crossed his arms angrily over his chest.

Sophia put her notepad down and leaned forward, staring right at Andy. "As a woman, I appreciate that you and your employees look out for women. As a detective, I have to talk to everyone that remembers her and assume the worst until proven wrong. I'm sure you can understand that, right?"

He nodded and relaxed his posture. "I have security cameras," he volunteered. "I'll get you copies of everything you need."

"We appreciate that," I said. "Is there anyone else who might remember Grace, particularly from last night?"

"Jason, the bartender, might?" Andy offered. "He worked last night, and he's got a good memory. He's in the back prepping for tonight."

We headed toward the kitchen. I asked Sophia in a whisper, "What do you think? Is he our guy?"

"No," Sophia said firmly. "He wouldn't hurt a woman. He hates men as much as most women do."

I nodded in agreement as I pushed through the swinging door to the kitchen. We found Jason standing at a stainless-steel table, knife in hand. He quickly worked through a pile of limes, cutting them into garnish wedges.

"Jason, can we have a word?" I asked.

Jason didn't turn. I glanced at Sophia.

"Jason," Sophia said louder. When he still didn't turn, she tapped him on the shoulder. "Sir, I—"

Jason turned quickly, slashing the air with his knife. Sophia jumped out of the way just in time. I reached for my holster but stopped when I saw the terrified look on his face.

"Holy shit," Jason said, yanking the earbud headphones from his ears. "I'm so sorry. I didn't hear you."

He held his hands up in surrender. His eyes grew wide when he realized he was still holding the knife, which he promptly dropped to the floor.

"Am I under arrest?" he asked, voice shaking.

"Should you be?" Sophia responded.

"No, of course not. I didn't hurt Grace."

"Yet you know exactly what we're here to talk about," I said skeptically.

Sophia stepped in. "Did you see Grace here last night?"

"I did. She came in every Saturday night, and sometimes during the week."

"Were you close with her?" Sophia asked.

"No, I wouldn't say that," he said. "I never met her outside of the bar. That big blonde hair is hard to forget, though."

"Take us through last night," Sophia directed. "What do you remember about Grace?"

"Everything was normal when she first got here. I made her a drink, she asked me about a class I am taking, then I told her to have fun. I knew she'd met someone when a guy asked me to make a fuzzy navel."

"How do you know that drink was for her?"

"It's what she always ordered," he snapped.

"Maybe he ordered it for some other girl?" Sophia suggested gently.

"Listen, this is beer country," he explained, rather annoyed. "I sell more Bud and Coors Light in one night than mixed drinks all year."

"Ok, fair enough," Sophia acquiesced. "Did the man happen to pay with a card that might have his name?"

"We're cash only," Jason said. "The owner doesn't believe in credit cards. Around midnight, though, Grace came to say goodbye and get her purse. The guy was behind her. She told me his name was Cass."

"That's an interesting name," I mumbled.

"Can you give us a description?" Sophia asked, ignoring me.

"He was average height, skinny, and his face was shaved clean."

"Have you ever seen him before?" I asked.

"I don't think so, but all the cowboys look the same after a while. He was dressed in all black, nothing fancy. Even his belt buckle didn't tell me anything."

"Excuse me for not being up to date on cowboy fashion," I said, "But what does that mean?"

He tried to hide his annoyance but didn't quite pull it off. "Half the cowboys here are on the rodeo circuit, so they wear their trophy buckles. The buckle shows their event, and you can tell a lot about a cowboy based on what event he rides. The rest are wannabe rodeo stars with huge, impractical buckles that we all know they found at a yard sale. But this guy," he paused, thinking, "This guy had a standard, square buckle. Like the one that came on the belt when he bought it at Walmart. It's like he woke up that morning and decided to play cowboy."

"It's not a crime to play dress up or pretend to be something you're not," Sophia pointed out.

"No, of course not." Jason was getting irritated. "But when most people go out, they try to stand out, right? Grace wore purple boots because they made her feel special. Every time she wore them, she showed them to me and said they were her lucky boots. Not this guy, though. This guy acted like he didn't want to be seen."

"Most bartenders aren't familiar with their customer's footwear," Sophia pointed out.

Jason rubbed his hands over his face in growing frustration. "Look, I'm usually invisible behind the bar. Guys throw their money at me to pay their tab but couldn't care less about me otherwise. And if girls give me any attention, it's to flirt with me, hoping I give them free drinks. When I don't, I become invisible again. That never happened with Grace, though. She shook my hand and introduced herself the first night she came here. She greeted me by name every night I worked and asked me how I was doing."

"It sounds like you were interested in her as more than a customer," I pushed.

"She was a genuinely good person. You can't deny that that's rare these days," he challenged.

I decided to push Jason and see if he got angry enough to give up some more information. "But maybe you wanted this rare girl for yourself? Maybe you saw her dancing with another guy and couldn't handle her wanting someone else?"

"Grace could have whomever she wanted. I knew she was looking for a boyfriend, and I hoped she would find one, but I didn't want it to be me."

"I find that hard to believe," I jabbed. "A strong, good-looking guy like you? How am I supposed to believe you weren't interested in a beautiful, kind young woman?"

His face hardened. "Because I'm gay."

I fumbled my pen. "Oh," was all I could say.

Sophia stepped forward and shook Jason's hand. "Thank you for your time, Jason. If we have any other questions, we'll call you."

I practically ran through the bar, trying to flee my embarrassment. Back in the sticky heat, I cursed at myself.

"You really put your foot in your mouth on that one," Sophia teased.

"I know, I know." I shook my head, then asked. "Any thoughts?"

"It's not Jason. We'll have plenty of witnesses and camera footage of him behind the bar all night. The murderer has to be a customer. With all the travelers that stop here, it'll be a miracle for us to get a name."

"Maybe we'll get lucky and get a license plate on the security cameras," I said.

"Let's hope we find something. Right now, we don't have much to go on. It'll probably take Andy a few days to get us the security footage. What else can we do tonight?" Sophia asked.

"Well, Cathy won't have any results until tomorrow. We should take the rest of the day off because it will be long days and late nights until this is solved."

Sophia nodded. "What are you going to do tonight?"

I smirked at her. "I'm going home to enjoy some dessert."

A Good Time to Lose

I took a break from traveling and returned to Omaha, NE, in 2017. I booked a flight for my favorite time of year, autumn. September is the sweet spot between the heat and humidity of summer and the frigid temperatures of winter. It is also football season, and the University of Nebraska-Lincoln Cornhuskers were about to start their campaign for another National Championship. The state was in a frenzy.

Football season also means a lot of great cooking competitions. Every week there were half a dozen contests to choose from: BBQ, chili, ribs, and any other type of food you could imagine. The only thing not represented was desserts, which I would've dominated with my new *patissier* skills. I signed up for as many as I could because, let's be honest, I'm a show-off and wanted to win some prizes.

The Nebraska Chicken Growers Association hosted a chicken wing cook-off. I prepared a sweet chili sauce that I had learned in Thailand. Hundreds of people tasted the wings and voted for their favorites. After the long, hot day, I was disappointed that I hadn't even placed. I began quickly packing my mini grill and kitchen supplies into the back of my truck.

Someone came up behind me and said, "You should've won." I turned to see a man standing under the canopy. He was tall and well-built, with beautiful dark eyes. He had long hair pulled back into a neat ponytail and a trimmed mustache. He was extremely handsome.

All I said to him was, *I know*, then continued cleaning my area. Without asking, he began helping me clean. We talked the whole time about nothing in particular, but in a comfortable manner. I didn't even wait for him to ask me for dinner; I just told him when to meet me at the best chicken wing joint in Omaha.

We must've seen greatness in each other because we married two years later! I still make my husband, Dawson, my sweet chili wings at least once a month. It's been three years, and he still thinks I should've won that day.

Sweet Chili Chicken Wings

PREP TIME: 1 hr 15 mins   COOK TIME: 25 mins
TOTAL TIME: 1 hr 40 mins   SERVINGS: 4 servings

INGREDIENTS
- 3 tablespoons canola oil
- ¼ cup rice vinegar
- 1 tablespoon, plus 2 teaspoons soy sauce, divided
- 4 cloves garlic, minced
- ½ teaspoon fresh ginger, minced
- 1 teaspoon chili oil
- ½ teaspoon fish sauce
- 3 pounds chicken wings
- ¼ teaspoon sweet Thai chili sauce
- 1 teaspoon hot sauce of choice

INSTRUCTIONS
- In large bowl, combine oil, rice vinegar, 1 tablespoon soy sauce, garlic, ginger, chili oil, fish sauce. Pour over chicken wings, tossing to coat.
- Cover and marinate for an hour.
- Place cooling rack in baking sheet and place chicken wings on top of cooling rack. (This allows air to flow around chicken)
- Cook 400° for 20 minutes, flip, and cook for an additional 20 minutes.
- While chicken cooks, mix remaining soy sauce, sweet chili Thai sauce, and hot sauce of choice (increase/decrease to taste). Heat in saucepan.
- Pour sauce over wings and toss. Add garnish if desired, serve warm.

Chapter 4

The story of Grace's murder broke on the local news channels on Sunday night. Monday morning, we were finally able to track down contact information for Grace's family and we spent all day on video chats with various family members. Her mother was taking her death particularly hard, as was to be expected, but her father was a rock. He hadn't shed a tear in all the hours we had talked with him. Neither Sophia nor I were shocked, but we knew, deep down, his daughter's death tore him up.

Unfortunately, they didn't have any information that would help us find Grace's killer. She hadn't told them about anyone new in her life, romantic or otherwise. She hadn't complained about her friends or anyone she worked with. Overall, Grace seemed as kind and genuine as Jason had stated. She didn't seem to have any enemies, which was good for her but left us with no suspects.

After a press conference given by Chief Probst on Tuesday morning asking for information on our possible suspect or Grace, calls flooded in from people claiming to know Grace. We cross-referenced names with the list of relatives we'd gotten from Mr. Whitmore and her Facebook friends list. We were able to weed out most of the calls as fakes looking for their fifteen minutes of fame on the evening news.

Several calls were legitimate, so we interviewed old college classmates or new coworkers on Tuesday afternoon. None of them ended up being helpful. They confirmed her character but didn't know who might have wanted to hurt Grace.

It was nearly 8:00 in the evening, and the sun was streaming horizontally through the windows. Sophia and I were tired and frustrated from a day of no answers to our questions. It was one of those days where we wished real-life investigations went more like a TV show: tests only gave good results, the first suspect was always the right one, and the case was closed in a day. But that's not how it works in the real world. Luckily, there was only one friend left on our list. I wasn't holding my breath that the interview would be a valuable use of our time.

"Grace Whitmore's friends are here," Sophia said.

"Friends? Plural?" I asked.

"Yes, three of them."

"There's only one name listed," I whined.

"That one decided to bring her friends because they are her *best friends ever.* You'll like them, though; two of them are very perky." She said the last three words with a dramatic valley girl voice.

"Is it too late to start drinking on the job?"

She smacked me on the shoulder. "Let's get this over with."

A uniformed officer had taken the three young women into an interrogation room. They were in one of the nicer rooms, with cushioned chairs and walls painted a soothing light blue. We saved this room for people we wanted to feel safe and comfortable talking to the police. I told Sophia to run the interview.

The three young women were seated on one side of the table. Two could have been twins: bleach blonde hair, manicured fingers, faces caked with makeup, and big, gaudy earrings. We asked their names.

"Aliviah," the first woman said, smacking her gum as she talked, "With an *A* at the front and an *H* at the end."

"And I'm Beylee with three *E*'s," the other one said, tapping the table with her fingers to emphasize each word.

I saw Sophia's death grip on her pen as she wrote out the names.

The third friend didn't volunteer her name. She sat quietly, keeping a watchful eye on the other two. She was what my sexist father would call "Walmart pretty." She had little makeup on, her hair was natural, and she was dressed for comfort, not fashion. But she was still pretty. I could tell she was the smart one of the group, the most mature. She was the one that was going to give us valuable information.

"Thank you for coming in, ladies," Sophia said. "I know this must be hard for you."

"It's been, like, *so* hard," Aliviah said.

"Yeah, so hard," Beylee agreed, her hand over her heart.

"Tell me, ladies," Sophia continued, "How well did you know Grace?"

"We were her *best friends*," Aliviah said. "We did everything together."

27

"Yeah, everything," Beylee parroted. "Shopping, hair, nails. All the important stuff, we were there for her."

"What do you mean by 'the important stuff'?"

Aliviah and Beylee looked at each other, confused, before Aliviah said, "We just told you: shopping, hair, and nails."

I caught the third friend rolling her eyes and wished I could, too.

"Have you ever gone to Barn Sour with Grace?" Sophia asked.

"A few times," Aliviah said, "Like, a few months ago."

"But not recently?"

"No," Beylee said, "It's not our crowd. The place is full of *cowboys*." She sneered her lip at the word.

"And you don't like cowboys?"

Aliviah scoffed at Sophia. "I mean, they're fine to look at, but—"

Beylee cut in. "—But we want men that fill out their business suits and bank accounts—"

"Not their Wranglers!" They finished together, giggling like teenagers.

The third girl put her hand over her face. Embarrassed or disgusted, I wasn't sure. Either would be justified.

"What can you tell us about her besides her beauty routine?" Sophia asked testily.

Aliviah and Beylee looked at her in utter confusion. "What do you mean?" Beylee asked.

"Do you know if she liked her job? Who else did she spend time with? What were her hobbies?" Sophia pushed.

The girls looked at each other and stuttered, obviously struggling to think of an answer to any of the questions. The conversation didn't improve, despite Sophia trying to get information for over thirty minutes. The third friend scoffed, mumbled, and clenched her fists. I was worried she was going to hit or strangle Aliviah and Beylee.

"All right, I think we're done here," I interrupted firmly when I could tell Sophia was about to launch herself across the table. "Thank you again, ladies. If you think of anything else that might be helpful, please call us."

Sophia continued scribbling in her notebook. I glanced down and saw the word USELESS in all caps and underlined. I nudged her to get her attention, then glanced at the third friend. She nodded in understanding.

"Ma'am," I said to the third friend. "We need you to hang back a second. We need your name for the records. The other two can see themselves out."

She didn't seem convinced, but she sat back down. "My name's Jill. Just Jill. No weird spelling."

"We appreciate that. We see some atrocious names nowadays," I said.

"Like Beylee with *three E's*?" she asked.

We both smirked, and I could feel her soften a little.

"Let's be honest," I said, "The only thing crazier than how they spell their names is their idea of 'important' things."

"I'm glad I'm not the only one that thinks that," she said.

"I'm sorry if this seems inappropriate, but why are you friends with them," Sophia asked. "They seem awful. You don't strike me as someone that *needs* people, so why are you friends with them?"

"I'm not their friend. I'm Grace's friend, and *she's* friends with them. They call me her bodyguard."

"Why is that?" I asked.

"Because I always made sure those two idiots weren't taking advantage of Grace. She had the purest heart of anyone I knew. She would give you the shirt off her back. Not literally, because she was too modest, but she would buy you a shirt if you needed one."

"And people took advantage?" Sophia guessed.

"Yes. All the shopping and hair and nails? Grace paid for it. Her parents are wealthy, so she didn't mind. But she couldn't see when people were using her. No matter how many times I tried to tell her." She shook her head, angry at whatever she was thinking. "Those two don't care about her. They only called you because they liked the drama of being friends with a murder victim. They're disgusting."

"Why did you come with them?" I asked. "You didn't seem interested in talking to us while they were here."

"I came with them to make sure they didn't embellish. I knew they would lie to you to make a better story or to make themselves look like victims. In the car, I told them I'd call them out if they tried anything. I also mentioned that lying to police is called obstruction of justice and they'd be thrown in jail. I'm not sure if that's true, but they bought it."

"It's not quite that simple, but it was a smart play on your part," I said.

Jill smiled at the compliment.

"Wait, you rode with them?" Sophia asked.

"I *drove* them. They can't put their cell phones down long enough to drive. No way I was going to put my life in their hands."

29

"Smart thinking," I said. "Tell me what you know about Grace."

"Grace was too nice for her own good," Jill said matter-of-factly. "When we worked together waitressing during college, she helped others when she knew they wouldn't return the favor. Aliviah and Beylee aren't the only friends that have used her as a cash cow. She was attracted to trashy guys, too. She thought she could love them enough to save them from themselves. Luckily, she usually figured out pretty quickly that they couldn't be helped and would break up with them."

"Could any of these men be responsible for her murder?" I suggested.

"Not likely," Jill said. "She was so sweet, even when she dumped them. It's like she convinced them that it was *their* idea that they broke up, that it's what *they* wanted. They always left on good terms."

"Grace was found in the parking lot. She had no drugs in her system and only had two drinks, so she wasn't incapacitated. Yet, she followed our suspect outside. Was it typical for her to take a risk like that?"

"No, Grace was always cautious when we went out. She never let us accept drinks from strangers or leave our drinks unattended. And she never allowed us to leave with a man." She gritted her teeth together, frustrated at a memory she wasn't sharing. "It caused some problems because she was so adamant about it."

"How so?"

"Earlier this year, we went out to a club downtown. I was the DD, so I wasn't drinking. I met a guy there, and we hit it off. I told her I was going outside to have a cigarette with him, and she freaked out. She said she wouldn't let me go anywhere alone with him. I told her she wasn't my mother, and I could make my own decisions, but she wouldn't listen. I finally told her that I was going home with the guy, and she could find a different ride home."

"Did you leave with him?" Sophia asked.

"No, of course not," Jill snipped. "I'm not stupid. I left alone. I went home. I just wanted to prove a point to her. I appreciated her being protective, but at the end of the day, I'm an adult and can do whatever I want."

"This guy you met; did he see Grace? Maybe he had some resentment toward her for getting in his way. Maybe he ran into her on Saturday night and decided to get revenge?"

"He saw her, but it couldn't have been him on Saturday night."

"You sound certain," Sophia challenged.

"I am. He was with me at my parents' house for family dinner," Jill replied.

"We started dating a few weeks after we met. He's met Grace several times since then, and she apologized for her behavior. They got along well."

"Did you ever go to Barn Sour with her?"

"I went with her all the time in college," she said. "Since we graduated, though, I've had too much on my plate. Between my family obligations and starting a new career, I don't have the time or energy to go with her."

"Do you know if there was anyone she was regularly seeing? Or someone that she was specifically going to see?"

"No, she would've told me. She was playing the odds that if she went enough, her 'true love' would find her." For the first time, her eyes filled with tears.

"The only description we have of a possible suspect is 5'6"-5'10", slight build, short hair. Does that sound like someone you recognize?"

"Sounds like half the men I know," she said. "Except for my guy, he's tall and thick. So, it couldn't be him even if he wasn't with me."

We thanked Jill for her time and escorted her to the door.

"Jill," I called. "No one would blame you for never seeing Aliviah and Beylee again now that Grace is gone. Might be a good time for a clean break, yeah?"

"One step ahead of you, Detective," she said with a wicked grin, "I'm not even giving them a ride home."

* * * *

Wednesday was a rainy, gloomy day. August is usually a dry, hot month, but this year it was a wet, hot month. But, as every Nebraskan will tell you any time it rains, we needed the moisture. But I hated being wet. I took an extra pair of socks and dress shoes with me in case I stepped in a puddle. The whole drive to work I hoped Sophia and I wouldn't be called into the field. I just wanted a quiet day of paperwork and reviewing case notes.

At 10:30, Chief Probst's assistant dropped a small package at my desk Wednesday afternoon. Sophia reached across her desk to mine and snatched it up.

"Hey! That was delivered to the man in charge!" I said incredulously.

"Well, when he shows up, you let me know," she quipped, tearing open the package with her teeth.

She tipped the package, and a blue flash drive fell into her palm. It was

31

labeled BARN SOUR.

"It's about time!" Sophia exclaimed. "Let's go watch some security footage."

In the war room, we looked at the table of evidence. We had the cast iron skillet with the lab report confirming that the blood and hair were Grace's. Pictures from the autopsy and crime scene were scattered around. The toxicology reports were all negative except for a reasonable blood alcohol level for the two fuzzy navels we knew she'd had.

Sophia inserted the flash drive into a laptop. When everything was downloaded, we saw hundreds of videos. We'd only requested footage from a week before the murder, but it seemed like Andy Andrews had gone back almost a month. Each video had a different thumbnail with a file number corresponding to the camera number, the date, and the hour the clip started. Sophia and I gawped at each other incredulously.

"That's a lot of footage," she whispered. "I'll take the outside, and you can take the inside?"

"Let's get to it," I sighed.

There were ten cameras in total. Sophia had three outside: one catching the whole length of the porch and the front door and two facing out into the parking lot. Inside, I had seven to go through: one behind the bouncer, one facing the bar, one in the prep room, one outside the bathrooms, and three scattered through the dance hall. There were surprisingly few blind spots. The footage was black and white and slightly grainy. It wasn't crystal clear like I see in TV shows, but it wasn't the worst security footage I'd ever seen. At least I could make out the basic features of everyone that stepped into view, even if the details were fuzzy.

I clicked on the camera that was behind the bouncer. It showed the back of his head and pointed toward the people coming in the front door. At 9:37, I saw Grace's big, blonde hair enter the door. She talked with the bouncer before he waved her through. I tracked her through the building to the bar. She flagged down Jason, the bartender. He brought her the fuzzy navel and they talked for a few minutes. I noted her extending her leg and pointing at her purple boots. It all played out just as Jason had said.

I ran the footage at double speed as she danced. At 10:22, Grace disappeared from view. I stopped the reel and rewound it to the last sight of her hair. I saw her trip, her hair swishing behind her as she fell. But she didn't hit the floor. Someone caught her. He must have been wearing all black because I couldn't identify any features. There was just a black void in the film. I knew it was a person and not a glitch on the video because I could see his pale hands. This had to be the man-in-black Jason described.

I followed the dark shape as he walked to the bar. He paid for their drinks with cash. Though our standard toxicology screen showed Grace hadn't been drugged with any of the usual substances, I watched the video repeatedly to see if he had slipped her something. There were drugs we didn't routinely check for or were undetectable. But he'd had to hold the glasses above his head as he pushed through the crowd, so there was no way for him to have spiked her drink.

I clicked on another camera, which caught a wider angle of their meet cute. When he set her on her feet after catching her, I noted that the man didn't appear much taller than Grace. When I considered the heels on Grace's boots and the four inches her hair added to her height, our mystery man appeared to be around 5'6". I couldn't tell much else in the darkness.

From 10:24 until midnight, I followed her and the man in black around the venue. At 12:09 am, Grace and the man went to the bar, collected her purse, and left the dance hall. The bouncer's hall was well-lit, so it had better footage to verify the height and general build of the suspect. Unfortunately, the camera was at their backs, so I couldn't see his face.

I glanced at my watch. It had already been three hours. In all that time, I hadn't gotten much viable information. I couldn't get a clear shot of the man's face from any angle. Our description was spot on. He was a good line dancer, too. He also appeared to be a gentleman and made Grace feel special—right up until that part where he smashed her in the head with a cast iron skillet.

"I don't have anything good inside," I told Sophia. "Just confirmation about what we already know. I could barely see anything because of his black outfit. Everything Jason told us was true, too, based on the footage. They went outside at 12:09."

"Way ahead of you," Sophia said. "I caught them walking out, and our guy looks about 5'7", give or take an inch. The other two cameras are on two corners of the building. It gives us views of the whole parking lot. The dumpster was visible in the afternoon, but trucks started parking around it shortly after the bar opened. So, unless they move before our guy dumps her body, I don't think it'll help much."

"How far through the parking lot did you track them?"

"Not very far. An SUV almost runs them over just before they leave the camera's range. I lost them pretty quickly toward the back of the parking lot. The last shot is at 12:14. Both cameras have night vision, but headlights flare out the footage every time a car drives by. There is only one yard light clear at the back of the parking light, so it's too dark for the cameras to pick up anything useful past the first few rows of vehicles."

"Did you get a good view of our guy?"

"Nothing up close. His damn cowboy hat blocked his face. I didn't see a ponytail, though, so the short hair Jason mentioned was right."

"How about his truck? Any clues to what kind of truck he was driving?"

"No. But he didn't leave right away unless he drove out without headlights. I didn't see any vehicles leave the parking lot between losing them in the dark and the bar closing at 2:00 am."

"Damn." I rubbed my face with my hands, frustrated that we had spent more valuable hours getting nowhere again. "Sophia, boss me around. Tell me what my next move is."

"You're going to check traffic cams and CCTV footage from businesses around the bar," she said. "There are two traffic cams outside the driveway to Barn Sour. Track vehicles that turn into the driveway that evening and then cross off any that leave before 12:14. If we can figure out which vehicles are left in the lot when Grace leaves with our suspect and who owns them, maybe we can pull some DMV pictures to see if anyone matches our description. It's a long shot, but it might pay off."

"Yes, boss," I said sarcastically. "What are you going to do?"

"If I'm the boss," she said smugly, "I'm going to sit here and supervise you."

Murder and Cheesecake

While I was in Stockholm, Sweden, I worked at a very fancy 5-Star restaurant. I felt animosity toward me when I started at the restaurant. Even after proving I was competent in the kitchen, the tension didn't ease.

I realized that the issue wasn't my cooking. It was because I didn't speak their language. Most Swedes speak English as a second language, so they *could* talk to me, but I could tell it was frustrating for them to have to translate for a foreigner. I knew I had to learn their language in order to be accepted.

I struggled until I met my biggest ally in the kitchen, Elias. He was a confident, gifted young chef. He helped me learn the Swedish words for everything we used in the kitchen. When an order was called, he would point at the ingredient or tool I needed and say the Swedish word. He was firm about me remembering the words, but never demeaning.

Within a month, my "work words" were so good that Elias tested me by giving me instructions in Swedish for Ostkaka Cheesecake. The first cheesecake didn't turn out well. Somehow, I mixed up the words for salt and sugar—which is embarrassing because the Swedish word for salt is *salt*. I got it on the second try, though!

After that, Elias started teaching me conversational words. Our talks were stilted at first, but I loved our chats about our lives. When I felt more confident, I organized a group outing with some of the other restaurant staff. They were hesitant at first, but with Elias's encouragement, they agreed to come.

Stockholm has a famous murder mystery tour that I was dying to try. Eight of us set out on a cool morning to solve the Murder at the Royal Palace. We were given one clue and a map, and I surprised them all by being able to read the instructions on the clue. I didn't read it fast and was corrected on a few of the words, but overall, I did well. I received praise and hugs before we set off through Stockholm to try and solve a murder.

The mystery proved to be very challenging but very fun. We walked several miles as I read the clues. Within hours, we had solved the case, saved the Royal Family, and become a team. That was the first time I felt like I was being accepted by my coworkers. We could talk more freely now that I knew more of their language, and I owed it all to Elias. In his honor, here is his Ostkaka Cheesecake recipe.

Swedish Ostkaka Cheesecake

PREP TIME: 10 mins
TOTAL TIME: 1 hr 10 mins

COOK TIME: 1 hr
SERVINGS: 6 servings

INGREDIENTS

- 2 eggs
- ¼ cup sugar
- ¼ cup almond flour
- 3 tablespoons rice flour
- 1 cup half-and-half
- 1¼ cup cottage cheese

INSTRUCTIONS

- Lightly grease 8-inch round cake tin or ceramic dish.
- Whisk eggs and sugar until smooth.
- Add almond flour, rice flour, half-and-half and cottage cheese to mix.
- Pour mixture into tin.
- Bake at 350° for 1 hour until lightly browned on top.
- When cheesecake is almost finished baking, add toppings of choice.
- Remove from oven and allow to cool. Serve warm or lukewarm.

Chapter 5

I spent several more hours going through endless traffic camera footage, logging each make, model, and color of vehicle that turned into the driveway. It would've taken me even longer, except that one of the traffic cameras had been removed for repairs the week before the murder, so we missed any vehicles turning into the driveway from the east.

While I was busy with that, Sophia watched the rest of the footage from Saturday night. She saw our suspect enter the bar at 6:47 pm. That early in the evening, there was no line to get in, so he wasn't in view of the porch camera very long. She didn't get a look at his face in the bouncer's camera, either. Inside, he found a table at the back of the dance hall and dis-appeared into one of the few blind spots.

When she had exhausted that idea, she went back farther and started watching the older security footage of the bar's front porch. We hoped our suspect had been to Barn Sour before, which would give us more options for vehicles, witnesses, or other potential victims.

"So, if our guy hasn't been to Barn Sour in the last month, it means he's not a regular," Sophia pondered. "So, the chances of him seeing Grace there before is slim, right?"

"Right," I agreed. "Does that mean the suspect saw her elsewhere and tracked her to Barn Sour? Or was it a coincidence that he found her there on Saturday?"

"That's an excellent question, Detective," she teased. "A good question to think about more tomorrow. Let's get out of here."

"It's past 10:00," I scolded playfully. "I'm never going to let you be the pretend boss again if you're going to make me work overtime."

"We both know it's only a matter of time before Chief makes me the boss anyway, and there won't be anything you can do about it!"

I struggled to stay awake on the drive home. The streets were wet with the unseasonal rain that had fallen most of the day. The patter of the slow, steady drizzle hit my windshield, and the rhythmic sweep of the windshield wipers tried to lull me to sleep. I had to turn my air conditioner on high and crank the radio to stay conscious.

When I finally pulled into the garage and climbed out of my car, I had to lean on Harper's little forest green truck for support. All I wanted to do was crawl into bed and cuddle with Harper.

I opened the door from the garage into the mud room and was greeted with a glorious sight: Harper, standing naked next to the front-load washing machine. I was so mesmerized by her beautiful face and perfect body that my car keys and briefcase slipped from my fingers, clattering onto the floor.

"The spin cycle is about to start," she said in that hungry tone I knew so well.

I reached her in two steps. We kissed furiously as I touched her all over her body. She tugged at my tie and belt, unable to get my clothes off fast enough. When the washing machine started to shake, I grabbed her under her perfect ass and lifted her onto it. We finished just before the spin cycle ended.

I leaned against Harper's bare chest for a few minutes, completely exhausted. She ran her hands through my hair and told me about her day. When the washer's buzzer sounded, I left Harper on top while I moved her clothes from the washer to the dryer.

"Why are you doing laundry so late?" I asked.

"I got drenched when I left the restaurant tonight," she explained. "I didn't want my clothes to get smelly in the hamper, so I just threw in a whole load."

I turned the dial on the dryer, pushed the start button, and lifted Harper down. She slid seductively down my body. I grabbed my clothes from the floor and put them in the hamper beside the washing machine.

Harper wrapped her arms around me and said, "There's nothing sexier than a man that helps around the house without being asked."

I laughed and let her take my hand and lead me to the bedroom. She slid a red silk negligée over her head and climbed into bed. I pulled on a pair of Ironman boxers and followed her. I wrapped my arms around her and pulled her close to me, our bodies forming together. I was drifting off when Harper turned to face me. She reached one arm around me and gently stroked her fingernails up and down my back. I shivered at the sensation.

"Do you think you and Sophia will be working late again tomorrow?" she asked.

"I hope so, but probably not."

"You hope you have to work late?" she asked in the dark.

"If we get a break in the case, we will probably work late," I explained. "If we don't, we won't have anything to do, so we'll be done early. So, I hope we work late because it means we are solving the case."

She nodded against my chest. "If you guys don't get a lead and you think you'll be home at a decent time, invite Sophia for supper. It's been a while since I've seen her. I want to catch up with her."

"You just saw her on Sunday," I reminded her.

"Yeah, but in girl friend time, that's basically a year!" she teased. "I'll let her know in the morning, though. What's on the menu?"

"I haven't decided quite yet. Would you rather have liver and onions or German borscht?"

"I think I'd rather order a pizza," I said.

"I'm pretty sure I remember our vows saying: in sickness and health, for richer or poorer, and you have to eat anything I cook or you can starve instead," she said.

"Hmm, I think that was someone else's wedding."

She kissed me deeply, then said, "Are you willing to risk it?"

"No, I am not," I said. "Not one little bit."

* * * *

On Thursday, Sophia and I spent seven hours searching for vehicles that could have belonged to our suspect. Of the vehicles we could see entering the lot, we saw most of them leave either on the traffic camera or by cross-referencing the exterior security footage. I had a list of dozens of vehicles that we never saw leaving the parking lot that became potential getaway cars.

Running the make and model through DMV records turned out to be a fool's errand. We thought we might get a few matches of each vehicle. We didn't account for the fact that very few vehicles had readable license plates due to the mud caked on the front and rear bumpers. Without the plate number, we could only search by color, make, and model, often resulting in over twenty similar vehicles in a 300-mile radius.

We tried to narrow the search based on the registered owners, too. We ruled out any vehicle registered to a woman. Unfortunately, that was a small portion of the drivers. We had to go through the rest individually, looking for drivers with similar height and weight as our suspect.

At 5:00, I slammed my laptop shut and groaned. My eyes were so dry and gritty from looking at the screen that I wondered if I had forgotten to blink for the last five hours. I was too tired to focus, especially since we weren't getting anywhere in the investigation. If we were, I would've pushed through.

"I'm calling it, Sophia," I said. "My eyes aren't working anymore and I'm just wasting our time."

"Me, too," she agreed, standing up and stretching. "I was just waiting for you to crack first."

I rolled my eyes. "See you at my place at seven?"

"I'll be there," she said. "I'm just going to run home and change. I'll bring another bottle of that cabernet Harper likes."

"She'll love that." As an afterthought, I said, "Feel free to bring some-one. A friend or whatever."

She didn't say anything, just waved over her shoulder as she walked out the door. Sophia rang our doorbell at 7:00 on the dot. She came alone, shoving the wine bottle in my hand before marching past me to the kitchen, where Harper was still working on supper. I uncorked the bottle, poured Sophia and Harper each a glass, then sat quietly at the island. Instantly, Harper and Sophia began chatting.

Sophia and Harper were friends, which was unusual for our situation. Most of the time, when cops of the opposite sex are partners at work, there is some animosity between the spouses and the partners. I blame Hollywood and the constant portrayal of cops as philanderers that do more on a stakeout than drink cold coffee. Partners becoming romantically involved happens so rarely that spouses shouldn't worry, but they still do. Regardless, it was never an issue for Sophia and me.

It had never even crossed my mind to cross that line with Sophia. For starters, I am madly in love with Harper. Secondly, our friendship felt so natural. From Sophia's first day on the job, we fell into a comfortable, easy routine like we had been friends for years. We had the same sense of humor, liked the same movies and bands, and preferred her to drive our unmarked car.

I was nervous the first time I invited her out with Harper and me. Harper had never been a jealous woman, but she had never had reason to be, either. I had no female friends, and all my previous partners had been men. If Harper hadn't liked Sophia, work- and home-life would have been awkward and difficult.

But I was wrong to worry. Sophia and Harper hit it off just as Sophia and I had. They've become good friends. They often go to lunch without me and text throughout the day. They even go shopping together, which gets me out of doing it. They quickly developed that unspoken language women have with each other, where they can communicate about stupid men without saying a word. I'd even caught Sophia putting her head in Harper's lap during one of their movie nights.

Maybe I should be worried about them *hooking up*, I thought.

The image of tall, lean Harper and petite, curvy Sophia wrapped in each other's arms floated through my head. It surprised me so much that I choked on my beer. I sputtered and coughed but waved away Harper's help before rushing to the bathroom. Once I had stopped coughing, I changed into a clean shirt and returned to the kitchen.

"Are you okay, honey?" Harper asked.

"Yeah, yeah, I'm fine," I said, my voice raspy. "Just a little beer down the wrong tube."

Sophia shook her head in mock disgust. "Imagine being so bad at something you've been doing your whole life. Swallowing must be tough for you."

"Now, now, Sophia," Harper chastised. "Don't be too hard on him. We both know it's women that are pressured to swallow."

"Harper!" I was shocked. "Don't say that to her! She doesn't want to hear about our sex life."

"Right, sorry dear," Harper said.

And there it was! That look! The way Harper glanced sideways at Sophia, her eyes slightly narrowed, her eyebrows raised a fraction, and her lips in a pursed smirk. Sophia saw it, too, and nodded in agreement.

What could that look mean?

"If you two are going to gang up on me, I'm going to watch the start of the boxing match."

"Sure," Sophia said, "Just leave the women to prepare the meal. How archaic of you."

"Nice try," I shot at her playfully, "Harper doesn't allow me to help when she cooks."

They laughed as I left the room. I plopped into my recliner in the living room and reached for the TV remote. It was sitting on top of a stapled packet of papers, with the words *Food and Adrenaline* at the top. It was an intro to a recipe in Harper's cookbook.

Harper had been working on her cookbook for almost eight months and thinking about writing it for even longer. She loved buying cookbooks written by her favorite chefs. On one of our first dates, she told me she had dreamt of writing her own cookbook. Harper wanted to tell stories about all the people that had influenced her cooking. She knew she owed much of her career to their teaching and inspiration and wanted to repay them.

For Christmas, I gifted her a new laptop with all the best software for writing, formatting, and marketing her cookbook. She planned on self-publishing the book, printing just enough copies to give to her friends and colleagues. She didn't imagine she could make a cookbook of the same caliber as Gordon Ramsey or Julia Child. She had herself convinced it would be good enough to have her friends' support, even if no one else cared. But I knew her better than that. I knew she wanted everyone to love her and admire her cooking.

Everything changed when she appeared on Omaha's morning news program, *Wake Up Midwest!* The hosts raved about her food and told her she needed to make a cookbook because everyone would want her recipes. She mentioned she was working on one, and the crowd went wild. The hosts both said they wanted copies.

The same night, people came into the restaurant asking to buy her cookbook. When Harper told them it wasn't finished, they offered to prepay. Of course, Jean-Pierre jumped in and started managing the orders and the money. Within a week, 150 copies had already been sold. The next week, one of the top cookbook agents from New York City called Harper, begging to represent her.

There were only six weeks until the deadline to complete the manuscript. The publisher had already finished all the pictures of the dishes Harper had picked. All she had to do was finalize the introductions for each recipe. Each one paid homage to the person who taught her the dish.

I have always been adamant about helping Harper any way I can. Whether she has a new idea or sets a new challenge for herself, I was the first to ask how I could help. This time wasn't any different. My job was to read the intros and give Harper honest feedback.

At first, there were only one or two here and there, which I read quickly and enjoyed. Then she started writing faster and would hand me five or six intros at a time. Between work and helping her at the restaurant, I started falling behind. Right now, there was an inch-thick stack in my bedside table drawer of intros I hadn't read. To make things worse, I was hiding it from Harper that I hadn't finished them.

This intro was for a Greek recipe she learned from an older man who owned several restaurants in the Greek Isles. He joined her on her many daredevil adventures when they weren't working. I was happy to know she'd had someone to share that passion with. I knew she hadn't always had that. That was a resounding theme in all of Harper's recipe intro-ductions: she made deep, meaningful connections with people.

My thoughts drifted back to Harper and Sophia. They had the same deep connection and friendship that never needed explanation or justification. I was happy Harper had someone like that in her life besides me. I was also happy Sophia had someone as well. Sophia never talked about any other friends. She never mentioned going on dates, either, let alone dating someone. It didn't make sense to me that she didn't seem to have anyone except Harper and me in her life.

In my opinion, Sophia was the whole package: smart, witty, funny, and kind. She was only 30 but had already accomplished so much in her career. On top of all of that, Sophia was beautiful, too. She had big brown eyes, olive skin, long, jet-black hair, and feminine curves. I couldn't think of any reason why men weren't falling all over her.

Personality-wise, Harper and Sophia were very similar, but physically they couldn't be more different. Harper was tall for a woman, slender, and had very few curves. She was deceptively strong, with arms toned from years of knife work and lifting heavy things in the kitchen. Her perfect pale skin made her look younger than 35. And I knew that she had men falling all over her.

Arms wrapped around my shoulder. "What do you think?"

My mind went blank as Harper's lips brushed my ear. "About what?"

"My story," she whispered seductively.

"It's amazing," I said, blood rushing away from my brain.

"Good," she whispered. "Supper's ready. Let's eat."

I made a mental note to finish reading the intro but forgot to save the note when I saw the food on the dining room table.

"Steak fajitas with three peppers, Mexican rice, refried beans, fresh guacamole, and homemade tortilla chips. And for dessert, I've got homemade

43

churros in the oven."

An hour later, Sophia pushed her plate away and rubbed her full belly. "Harper, you've outdone yourself again. That reminds me of the meals my grandma used to make, except better!"

"I'm glad you liked it, but don't go telling people that I'm upstaging grandmas. If word got around, grandmas would revolt against me."

"Your secret is safe with me," Sophia said, miming zipping her lips and throwing away the key.

"Wha's yo fa-rit meaw," I said through a mouthful of chicken.

Harper looked at me, disgusted, and said, "Are you five years old? You should know better than to talk with your mouth full."

"Sowwy." I choked down the bite, then repeated, "What's your favorite meal?"

"That's easy," Sophia said. "Chicago deep-dish pizza."

"That's not very original," I teased.

"Chicago Italians have made the best pizza since the 1940s," she argued. "We are famous for it for a reason."

Harper took another sip of her wine. "I've never been to Chicago, but I've heard the pizza is the best."

"I've tried every pizza place in the tri-county area, and none of them make a decent pie. They aren't bad pizzas, but they aren't Chicago deep-dish. I tried making one at home, but the crust tasted horrible. I even bought one of those fancy pizza cutters," she mimed the rocking motion of using a long curved-edge pizza blade. "I didn't even get to use the damn thing! And it's so big it doesn't fit in any of my drawers, so I had to hang it on a hook on the kitchen wall!"

I pointed a fork at her. "I've been telling you for months to get a bigger apartment. Then you'd have big enough drawers."

"That's one suggestion." She glanced at Harper, a sly expression on her face. "If only I knew an amazing chef that could whip one up."

"All right, all right, save your flattery for someone else," Harper chided. "I'll make you a deep-dish pizza the next time you come for supper."

"Do you promise?" Sophia said with pouty eyes.

"Cross my heart and hope to die," Harper said, winking at her.

"Aww, thanks, Harper. You're the best," Sophia said.

"I don't think it'll be as good as your grandma's, but I'll give it a go."

"Pizza is one of the few recipes my grandma wasn't very good at," Sophia corrected. "She never could get the crust to turn out right. I guess I have that in common with her."

"It sounds like you were pretty close to your grandma," I said.

"I was. My mom died in 2000. I was only eight, so I couldn't be left home alone. My dad was the lead detective in the Eastside Executioner investigation and was working 18-hour days. Grandma—my mom's mom—came to live with us until the case was solved."

I remembered the Eastside Executioner case. It had been one of my obsessions when I was in college for Criminal Justice. "I thought that case wasn't solved until 2010?"

"It wasn't," Sophia confirmed. "So, my grandmother's month-long visit turned into a ten-year stay. By then, we knew we couldn't manage without her. Grandma stayed with us until she died in 2018."

"I'm sure your father loved having his mother-in-law living with him," I teased.

"He didn't mind. They had a good relationship, and Grandma never nagged him about the long hours. She knew his job was important. And he was glad to have someone else to help with the woman stuff."

"It can be tough being a single parent," Harper said. "No one wants to have to do it alone."

"You're right," Sophia agreed. "And he did his best to be there for me for all the important things. Once, I had a championship volleyball game in the afternoon that he'd promised to be at. They were introducing the players when my dad showed up. He had been scuba diving in the Chicago River, searching for evidence. He was late, so he didn't change out of his scuba suit. He squeaked as he walked! But he made it, just like he promised."

I laughed. "That's one dedicated father. Ain't that right, Harper?" I looked at Harper, but she wasn't smiling.

I glanced at Sophia, who was glaring at me. "I'm sorry, Harper," Sophia said. "I didn't mean to go on about my dad like that."

I realized what was bothering Harper. She grew up in the foster care system, shuffled from home to home, more than thirty of them by the time she aged out of the system. In several of the homes, she had been abused and neglected. She didn't like to talk about it, even to me. When I saw the repulsive look on Sophia's face, I realized that she knew about it, too. I leaned in to comfort Harper, but she pushed me away.

"It's ok. I'm okay," Harper insisted. "Sophia, I don't want you to feel like you can't talk to me about your parents just because I didn't have any. Any good ones, at least."

"Have you met either of your biological parents?" Sophia asked gently.

"My mother overdosed when I was just a few months old. I'm grateful she stayed clean while she was pregnant with me, but she got high as soon as she got me home from the hospital," she said. "I've met my father a few times. He would pop back into my life every few years, swearing he would get sober and get me back. I stopped getting my hopes up before I turned ten, and by the time I was fourteen, I refused to see him."

"Have you ever thought about reconnecting with him now that you're an adult?" Sophia asked. "Maybe he's different? I know I'd love another day with my dad."

"No, never. Not even for our wedding," Harper said firmly.

I wrapped my arm around her. "And I have always supported that decision."

"I know you have," she kissed me gently, then leveled a severe look at Sophia. "There's a big difference between wanting more time with a man that loved you enough to wear a scuba suit in public and making time for a man that never made time for me."

Sophia bowed her head. "You're right. I'm sorry," she said. "I didn't mean anything by it."

Harper reached across the table for Sophia's hand and gave it a reassuring squeeze. "I know you didn't, Sophia. Don't think anything of it. Now," she said, changing the subject abruptly, "Who wants dessert?"

Sophia and I raised our hands greedily. When Harper brought out warm, fresh churros and cream cheese icing, I couldn't stop a moan escaping my mouth. Harper flashed me a goofy grin, but Sophia curled her lip at me. I mumbled *sowwy* through a mouthful but continued inhaling the dessert.

When the churros were gone, Sophia wiped her hands and finished her drink. "A perfect way to end a delicious meal."

"I'm glad you liked it," Harper said. "I can get you the recipe if you want."

"How about I buy the groceries, and you can cook it?" Sophia suggested. "Deal!"

Despite the big meal, I was still hungry, so I continued working on the chips and dip. "This guacamole is amazing, honey. Why haven't you made it before? New recipe?"

"No, I've been using that recipe for almost three years now."

46

"No, I don't think so," I argued. "I'd remember guacamole this good."

Suddenly, the mood darkened. I looked at Harper, and her face was pinched. Then I noticed the muscles in her jaw clenching. That meant she was angry.

"For starters, Dawson," she snipped, "As the person that does 99% of the cooking in this house, I think you should trust me when I say that I have used a recipe before."

"You're right, Harper, I'm sor—"

"And secondly, you should know that I've had that recipe for three years because I got it on our honeymoon. We both loved it so much that it's the only recipe I use."

"I'm sorry, honey, I don't remember that part of our honeymoon."

"That's odd. Last week you read my intro for the guacamole recipe that described why it was so important to me. And you said you loved it."

I felt a chill run down my spine. I remember telling Harper that I liked the recipe intro called *You Guac My World*. But the name is the only thing I remembered. I wasn't able to focus on it because of a case. Now, she'd caught me in a lie.

Sophia coughed and wiped her mouth with her napkin. "I think I'm going to go."

"Thank you for coming, Sophia," Harper told her. "I'll see you out."

I sat at the table, my head bowed, and my hands folded in my lap. I didn't move. Harper rarely got mad at me, which was good because it meant our relationship was solid. The bad part was that I wasn't sure how best to handle the situation. I knew not to try and joke my way out of it, and that she wouldn't talk until she was ready. I had to sit here and bide my time until she came to me. Then, we would talk this out, I'd apologize, and we would be happier after it was all done.

When she came back into the dining room, she silently started gathering the dishes and carrying them to the kitchen. When the table was clear, I followed her to the kitchen. I sat at the island, within reach but not in her way, as she loaded the dishwasher and wiped down the counter. When she was finished, she sat down beside me but didn't speak immediately.

She struggled to put her thoughts and feelings into words. Several times she opened her mouth to talk before snapping it back shut. Because of the traumatic childhood she'd experienced in the foster system, she learned early not to rely on anyone. She didn't trust men easily, and it had taken her a long

47

time to decide to trust me. I knew I had let her down, so I waited silently until she sorted everything and was ready to talk.

Finally, she said quietly, "You said you would help me."

"I know I did. I just—"

"You said you would help me with this cookbook," she said a little louder.

"I know I did. And I've tried, it's just—"

She held up a finger to hush me. "I need to know if you still want to help me. I need to know if you are with me on this. This is your one chance to get out of it. If you don't want to help, tell me now. I won't be mad. I won't hold it against you."

She meant it, too. She had never been one to lie about something like this and had never held a grudge. But the tears welling in her eyes told me she was scared that I would say I couldn't help her. The tears said that if I let her down this time, she'd never be able to ask me for help again. Big or small, she wouldn't allow herself to ask me for help and risk me letting her down like so many people had in the past.

I grabbed her hand, and she allowed me to hold it. "Harper, you know I'm proud of you for following your dreams. I am so sorry that I let you down. I do want to help you with your cookbook. Of course, I will help you. I will *do* better and *be* better for you. I promise."

A tear fell down her cheek, and I reached up to wipe it away. She let me pull her in for a kiss.

"I have a confession to make," I whispered.

She eyed me warily.

"I may or may not have had a little daydream about you and Sophia in bed together." I winked at her.

"You can daydream all you want, but consider yourself lucky that that will never happen," she said.

"Why is that?"

"Because, my love," she said, her face serious. "If Sophia and I got together, what would we need you for?"

You Guac My World

This recipe is near and dear to my heart because it involves my husband, Dawson. We were married in late 2019 and spent our honeymoon in Cozumel, Mexico, at a beautiful 5-star resort. I was about to open my restaurant, Clever Culinary, in Omaha, NE, and Dawson had just been promoted to Detective in the Omaha Police Department. We knew we wouldn't be able to go on a vacation for several years, so we went all out! Excursions, tours, fantasy suites, and fine dining every night.

I promised Dawson that I wouldn't ask for the chef or try to get into a kitchen, no matter how great the food was. I kept my promise until one particularly delicious meal. From the first bite of the creamy, smooth guacamole that topped my fish entre, I was obsessed. I raved about it for the whole meal. When the waiter brought the check, I asked him to tell the chef how much I liked the guacamole.

My husband is the type that befriends everybody. He's not the typical stoic cop that's portrayed on TV. So, I shouldn't have been surprised when *he* was the one that asked for a visit from the head chef. Despite my protests that I intended to keep my promise, Dawson convinced our waiter to introduce us to Chef Miguel.

I told Chef Miguel that his recipe was unique and special, but I couldn't figure out what the distinct flavor was. He was more than happy to help a fellow professional. Before I knew it, I was wearing an apron and helping Chef Miguel make his guacamole. (Turn to the next page for the special ingredient!)

Three hours later, I found Dawson sitting poolside, talking to an older couple about how they had kept their marriage so strong for over 30 years. It was the sweetest thing I had ever seen. He asked about the recipe, and I could tell he was genuinely interested, as he always was. I told him I would make it for him when we got home. The rest of the honeymoon, I focused on showing that wonderful man how much I loved him. And the rest of our lives, of course.

Creamy Guacamole

PREP TIME: 10 mins   SERVINGS: 4 servings

INGREDIENTS
- ¼ cup red onion, finely chopped
- 3 ripe avocados, peeled and seed removed
- 1 mango, finely diced **Special Ingredient**
- 2 tablespoons lime juice, freshly squeezed
- ¼ teaspoon fresh cracked black pepper

OPTIONAL INGREDIENTS
- ½ jalapeño pepper
- Additional 1 tablespoon lemon juice
- 1 teaspoon hot sauce of choice
- 1 tomato, remove seed and pulp, finely chopped

INSTRUCTIONS
- Smash onion, chiles, salt, and half of cilantro on a cutting board.
- Put mixture and juices in large bowl.
- Add remaining cilantro, avocado, mango, lime juice, and pepper.
- Mix to desired consistency.
- Include additional ingredients to taste.

Chapter 6
Callum McIntyre

It's hot. Too hot. Every year the Midwestern Scottish-Irish Festival was scheduled in August. Because why wouldn't you want the fairest-skinned, eastiest-to-sunburn people outside during the hottest time of the year with the harshest sun? It made no sense. Yet, here I am, for the third year in a row, covered in sweat and sunscreen from head to toe.

At least it's Saturday, Callum, I reminded myself.

I've been here since Wednesday, so I was tired physically and mentally. Saturday is always the most lucrative day, though. I made most of my money on this last full day of the festival, so I just had to push through. Saturday night is also the grand finale of the event, the Calling. It's an ancient tradition of Scottish clans that I've always enjoyed. So, I have that to look forward to, as well. Sunday would be an easy day of boxing up my goods and packing my SUV. Then, it was five days of sitting on the couch with a margarita watching *Downton Abbey*.

I've been a traveling salesman for the last five years. I started at home in Boston as an insurance salesman, then sold cable TV subscriptions. I tried to be a pharmaceutical rep, but doctors really are some of the worst people I've ever met, so I didn't last long there. Now, I work for a memorabilia company's United Kingdom division, traveling around the country and attending Scottish festivals.

I sell Clan memorabilia under my 20' x 30' plaid canopy. I have tables with mugs, hats, and wall hangings; spinning displays of jewelry and key-chains; and clothes racks with t-shirts, kilts, and scarves. Each item had the insignia and colors of dozens of Scottish clans. The items weren't authentic or purchased from Scotland but were unique enough that I didn't have to compete against other vendors.

The best part of this business is that I get to lean into my Scottish heritage. I always wear a T-shirt with Clan McIntyre's crest, and a modern kilt of my clan's tartan. The kilt is fun to wear and has plenty of pockets, but it helps me stay cool. Even a warm breeze up the kilt can cool the nether regions.

Last year, I got bored on a slow day at a festival in Utah, so I started talking to customers with a Scottish accent. Surprisingly, my sales increased when I started doing that. I've never been to Scotland, but I've watched plenty of movies. So, while I'm sure my accent wouldn't pass in Scotland, it was good enough to fool most Americans.

I'm a good salesman because I'm good at reading people and better at mirroring them. I can take one look at someone and figure out how to adjust myself to fit their personality. I can make myself meek and timid, or loud and boisterous, depending on how a customer acted. I can tell who needs to feel worshipped, who needs a straight-talker, and who wants to be flirted with. When I can cater to that need, they buy a lot more.

I saw a group of young ladies walking down the row between the booths. When they got closer, I called in my Scottish accent, "Come on over 'ere, lassies." I flashed a bright smile and beckoned them over.

The leader of the group made eye contact with me. She swished her hips as she came closer. I could tell she was used to having men interested in her body. It would never occur to her that she wasn't my type. I was only interested in her money, but I wasn't going to let her know that.

"My name's Callum. I'm just a young lad from Scotland, if you couldna tell from me accent. What's yer name?"

"I'm Bridget," the leader said. "And I'm from Omaha."

"This sure is a fine city here, Omaha," I pandered. "Tell me, Miss Bridget, where d'ya come from? Where does yer family hail from?"

"England," she said. "My grandparents came here from Birmingham."

"Oh, no! No England!" I put my hand over my heart, wounded. "Yer too *bonnie* to be descended from the bloody English."

"What does *bonnie* mean," she asked.

"Beautiful," I said with a wink. She blushed. "Why don't ye lasses have a look around. Christmas will be 'ere before ya ken it. I'm sure ye'll find summit special fer yer loved ones."

The women exchanged glances like they wanted to have a look, but the leader laughed and moved on to the next booth. They obediently followed.

Better luck next time, I thought with a shrug.

I busied myself straightening my tables and shelves while watching for potential customers coming down the aisle. Then, I heard a voice behind me.

"Does that ever work?" a man asked.

"What's that, lad?" I barely glanced at him. "Does what work?"

"That fake Scottish accent?"

I whipped around. "How dare ye call me accent fake—"

I stopped. Standing just inside the shade of my canopy was the most beautiful man I'd ever seen. And beautiful was the best word to use. He wasn't tall and thick like most men, but lithe, almost elfin. His short, dark hair was hidden under a black baseball cap. His shaved face was all angles, and he had the longest, thickest eyelashes I'd ever seen. When he smiled, my mouth went dry.

"I don't mean to be rude," he said. "But I spent a few years in the UK and I know that accent is fake."

"O' course, it's real! I dinna ken who ye think ye are, but—" He smiled at me again. Oh, that smile. I stepped closer to him and whispered in my Boston accent, "Yeah, it's fake, but I sell more if people think I'm from Scotland."

"Sounds like a shady sales tactic," he whispered back, thumbing through the clan hats.

"Only a little," I blushed. "I really am Scottish. And I'm proud of my heritage. The accent.... highlights that side of me."

He laughed. A beautiful song of a laugh. "Dinna fash," he said in the most convincing accent I'd ever heard, "Yer secrets safe wi' me."

It was my turn to smile. "Tell me, lad," I said without the accent, "Where does your family hail from?"

"Scotland, I just found out," he said. "My name's Cass, by the way."

He held his hand out to me, and I took it. "Callum McIntyre."

His hand was soft but powerful. An electric shock traveled up my arm. I didn't want to let go, so I didn't.

"It's nice to meet you, Callum." After a few seconds, he added, "Can I have my hand back?"

I dropped his hand immediately. "Sorry," I said sheepishly.

Cass continued browsing through my booth, coming around the table to peruse the clothing rack. He passed within inches of me several times, and I struggled to resist the urge to reach out to him. I was working up the nerve to start a conversation when an older couple approached my booth. I turned to them, praying that Cass wouldn't leave.

"How are ye folks doing on this fine summer day," I said. I noted that my fake Scottish accent was traveling a little West into an Irish accent. My nerves must be getting to me, but the couple didn't seem to notice.

"Wow, a real Scottish man," the pudgy husband said to his wife.

"O' course, I'm a real Scot and proud of it!" I said. "Especially on hot days like t'day. Since I dinna wear anythin' under me kilt, I 'ave a nice breeze keepin' me cool."

The man guffawed like all men do, and the woman giggled when I winked at her. I heard a chuckle behind me and caught a glimpse of Cass still perusing my goods. I was confident he was going to loiter until I could talk to him again.

Unfortunately, every Nebraskan and their kin chose that moment to stop by my booth. Suddenly, my tent was packed, and I had to do my best Scottish sales routine. I flattered the women, cajoled the men, and entertained the children. I was being called to all corners of the tent. I worried people would start walking away without buying anything. Or worse, without paying for what they took.

"Aye, ma'am, I'm from the Isle of Skye," said a familiar voice. "I spend me summers traveling your fair country with me brother and soaking up this bonnie sunshine. There's too much rain on the Isle."

I did a double take at Cass, who was under my canopy and talking to a customer. He smiled at me, then continued helping the lady.

"Aye, me brother and I make our livin' sharin' our heritage to the world." Later I heard, "Ah, no, we dinna look alike. I got me mam's *braw* features, but he got our da's bonnie singing voice. Like a canary, he is."

The next two hours flew by. Cass worked like he'd been doing this job his whole life. He could talk to someone for one minute and be able to recommend a product to them. I saw him ushering around several people with armloads of items. I stayed with the register, scanning and bagging items for all of the people that Cass helped.

After the rush died down, Cass and I stood side-by-side. My displays looked like a plague of locusts had come through, leaving empty rocks and hangers behind. It was a good problem to have, and I would've been overrun if it hadn't been for him. I wondered how I could repay him.

"You're right," he said after the rush died down.

I was confused. "About what?"

"That you owe me for helping you. You would've been overrun without me." He smirked.

I blinked dumbly. Did he just read my mind? "I could pay you?"

"Try again."

"I could give you something from my stock?" I suggested nervously.

"Not quite," he teased, and his stomach growled.

"I could buy you supper?" I took a last guess.

"There you go!" he exclaimed. "Get some shepherd's pie, maybe something to drink, and I'll meet you by the field entrance for the Calling. I know you want to go to that."

He patted me on the shoulder. As he stepped away from me, his hand trailed down my arm. His fingers lingered too long on my hand, and I felt like he wanted me to grab his hand. Before I could work up the nerve to do it, he left my booth and moved down the row of vendors.

What just happened? I asked myself. *Did I just get asked out on a date?*

I ran over the afternoon in my mind again and again as I restocked my booth. Cass was definitely sending me signals that he was interested in me. Why would he stick around all day otherwise? A great guy like him probably makes friends easily, but was he interested in more than friendship? I know I'm attracted to him, but was the attraction mutual? Was I overthinking the whole thing?

I have been out of the closet for almost five years now. My family is supportive, but I haven't had much luck dating. A few weeks ago, I met a guy through another vendor at Omaha's county fair. He'd brought me food for three days, and we seemed to hit it off. The last day of the fair, he asked me out the following weekend. I told him I wouldn't be back to Nebraska until the Scottish-Irish Festival, and after that I wouldn't be back for at least six months. I could tell he was disappointed. He promised to stay in touch, but he stopped answering my texts after that. He was the only person I'd connected with in over a year.

My mother has dementia, but before she forgot I was gay, she would ask me every time we talked if I had found a nice young man. When I said no, I told her it was because of my job. The travel has me in a new city every few weeks. The truth is that I'm just not good at dating. When I was in high school, the problem was that I was trying to date girls. Now that I'm trying to date men, I've learned that the problem is actually me.

It also doesn't help that I am not very good at telling who is gay. I pride myself on being able to read peoples' personalities, but their sexualities were another matter. These days, it's impossible to tell based on clothes, mannerisms, or how much makeup a guy is wearing. I'm terrified of incorrectly guessing a man's sexuality. So, if I don't find him in a gay bar, or he doesn't tell me specifically that he is gay, I assume he isn't. Hence, my hesitation to take Cass's invitation for a meal as a date.

When the vendor area was closed for the evening, I cleaned up my booth as quickly as I could. The more valuable items went into locked containers, then into the back of my SUV, which was backed up to the edge of my canopy. I tidied the rest, so it was ready for the morning. As soon as security gave the all-clear that all the visitors were gone, I zipped down the sides of the canopy for privacy. I counted the money in my cash register, put it in a vinyl bank bag, and then stashed it in a hidden compartment in my SUV. With everything secured and locked away, I left the vendor area.

I went to the nearest bathroom to freshen up. I lathered soap on my arms, face, and neck, washing away the dirt glued on by the sunscreen I'd applied throughout the day. I dunked my hair under the faucet, scrubbed as much dirt from it as possible, then patted it dry with thin paper towels. The red locks hung limp, but the curls would bounce back as they dried. My kilt still looked clean, and I hadn't dribbled any food on my shirt, so I was still presentable.

I stood back from the mirror and looked at myself. I've never considered myself an attractive man, but not an ugly one, either. My legs are too long for my torso, which was accentuated by my kilt. I was grateful I had red hair on my arms and legs, so I didn't look like a bear. My eyes are a dark blue pretty enough to detract people's attention from my big nose. Satisfied that I looked and smelled decent, I headed toward the food trailers.

The festival was divided into four sections. The vendor area had over 100 booths selling all types of goods, most of which had nothing to do with Scotland or Ireland. The exhibit area was set up for presentations, such as sheepdog trials and dancing competitions. The grandstand infield is where the Highland Games were held, as well as the Calling. The food court had trailers set up in a large circle, with picnic tables in the middle. The traditional foods were the most popular, but there were still lines for turkey legs, cotton candy, and trendy foods.

I didn't have to wait long at the shepherd's pie trailer, so I jumped in line for Scottish whiskey. A little liquid courage never hurt anyone, after all.

When I got to the grandstand, most of the seats were full. I searched the crowd but couldn't see Cass anywhere. I cursed myself for not getting his phone number or last name. After 10 minutes, I stalked to a trash can, poised to dump the food and return to my booth, when I heard a Scottish accent behind me.

"Aye, what's wrong wi' ya, tossin' out a perfectly good shepherd's pie? I've been slobberin' for hours jus' thinkin' about it."

I grinned at Cass. "I thought you stood me up."

"Of course not," he said in his regular, smooth voice. "I'm always looking for a handsome guy to spend the evening with. Come on; I saved us seats."

I followed him. I couldn't help but admire his small body. He wore loose black jeans and a black T-shirt. I don't know how he could stand the heat in all that black. He'd set a black messenger bag on the bench seat to reserve our spots. I handed him the fork and held out the plate of shepherd's pie. Without hesitation, he took a huge bite, his eyes rolling back in his head as he moaned in delight.

"Whiskey?" I offered, holding out one of the sipping glasses.

He took a small sip and nodded his head in approval.

"This hits the spot," Cass said.

"The whiskey or the pie?" I asked.

"Both," he said. "Try it."

"Shit, I didn't grab another fork," I said. I had been single for so long that it hadn't even occurred to me to get a second one. I pushed the plate at him. "You go ahead and eat it."

"Don't be silly. I promise I'm not sick. Cross my heart and hope to die." He drew an X over his heart and smiled at me.

I laughed at the childish gesture, but took the fork he offered.

When I hesitated again, he said, "This pie is the best I've had since I left Scotland. You don't want to miss out."

I gave in, grabbing the fork and helping myself to a big bite. He was right, it was delicious. I nodded and smiled, saying, "Is goot," through my mouthful.

He beamed. "I told you so. These mashed potatoes are amazing. Usually, they are too thick or I can tell they are out of the box."

"It sounds like you're a bit of a shepherd's pie connoisseur."

"More like a snob," he said after swallowing another bite. "Like I said before, I've spent time in the UK, primarily Scotland. I made a point to try all the traditional dishes while I was there. A well-made shepherd's pie is better than an orgasm if you ask me."

"I'm so jealous you've been to Scotland," I said. "I never have, but it's number one on my bucket list. What did you do while you were there?"

"I did everything. Of course, I started with the tourist traps: seeing castles, going to museums, things like that." He took another sip of whiskey. "When my vacation was over, I decided I wanted to stay. I needed money so I waitressed or did temp jobs I saw posted around whatever town I was in. No matter where I went, I always asked where I could get the best shepherd's pie. It was the first place I ate when I got to town, and the last place I ate when I left."

"You said you just found out you're Scottish?"

"I did one of those DNA ancestry kits. All my friends were doing them, so I thought I might as well join in. I was surprised when the results came in predominantly Scottish. I always thought I was German because of my very German-sounding last name. As it turns out, my family stole the name a few generations ago."

We polished off the shepherd's pie and talked while sipping the whiskey. Cass told me about his time in Scotland, including several Highland Games he'd attended.

"If you've seen the real thing in Scotland, why would you come here?" I asked. "I'm sure it's a crappy American-ized version of the real thing."

"This one is actually pretty accurate," he said. "Except that the Calling should technically be held *before* the games."

"What? Really?" I was genuinely shocked.

I'd seen the calling at hundreds of festivals over the last few years and it was always at the end. It never occurred to me that it should be done differently.

"Yes. In the olden days, before telephones and Twitter, if a clan chief needed help in battle, he would light torches to signal to all the outlying clans and allies. They would bring their men to the chief's castle before the battle. Then they would call out in front of everyone whether they would fight for the chief or not."

"They would travel *all* that way with *all* their men even if they weren't going to fight?" I asked. "Considering they didn't have motorized transportation back then, wouldn't it have been easier to just not show up?"

"You're not wrong, but honor was a big deal back then," he explained. "You had to show up and admit to everyone that you were a coward."

"Seems kind of harsh."

"Maybe, but that's the way it was done for hundreds of years. Until the clans were outlawed and forced to disband, anyways."

"I'll bet the Calling was moved to the end of the festival because it's a good closing spectacle," I said.

"I think you're right." Then, with the Scottish accent, "And no one fashes about betrayin' a thousand-year tradition if they ken it will increase ticket sales."

"I'll raise me glass to that, laddie," I said in my accent.

We tipped back the rest of our whiskey. I grimaced as it burned going down, but it turned into a smile when Cass reached for my hand. I stared into his eyes and felt myself leaning forward for a kiss. The trance was broken as bagpipes began playing, signaling the beginning of the Calling.

In the middle of the field, a giant stag made of wood and tinder stood on a platform ten feet in the air. A metal basin with a layer of kindling sat on the ground beneath it. From either side of the stag, fifteen clan chieftains marched single file onto the field. They held lit torches and wore their clan's tartan.

One at a time, each chief stepped to the basin and called out where the clan originated, their motto, and their most famous clan members. While their clansman in the crowd cheered in celebration, the chief dropped the torch into the basin. With each torch, the flame grew higher and higher.

I squeezed Cass's hand and said, "This is my clan," as Clan McIntyre's chief stepped forward.

"*Per ardua,* through hardship and difficulty," his voice rang out deep and clear. "We have persevered since the 14th century, through famine and war. From the western region of Argyllshire, we come. Proudest are we of kin Terence McIntyre, Royal Air Force Officer; Reba McIntyre, Queen of Country Music; and Drew McIntyre, professional wrestling champion. We are CLAN MCINTYRE!"

The crowd cheered as the chief added his torch to the basin.

The fervor of the crowd grew with each clan that was called to celebrate. The last clan chief placed his torch in the basin, and, within seconds, the stag caught fire. As all the flames came together, so did the clans. In unison the chiefs called out the motto of Scotland, *Nemo me impune lacessit!* The crowd joined in with the English translation, *No one provokes me with impunity!* The sound was deafening.

As the stag burned, the visitors began leaving the grandstand. Cass and I sat and talked, oblivious to the crowd. Cass told animated stories, gesturing wildly with his hands, leaving my hand empty and cold. Without fail, though, he always laced his fingers back into mine. Each story brought us closer, emotionally and physically. Our faces were almost touching when a member of the clean-up crew told us to leave. We glanced around and realized we were the only ones left in the stands.

"Can I walk you to your car?" I asked Cass.

"No," he said with a sly smile. "But you can walk me to your booth."

I blushed at his forwardness but took his hand when he offered it. We didn't stop talking as we wandered through the booths back to my enclosed canopy. I unzipped the side flap and let him in. I slowly rezipped the flap; the butterflies in my stomach needed time to settle. I wasn't sure what I was expecting from Cass—or myself. I unlocked the back of my SUV and began digging through the mess.

"Do you sleep in your car?" he asked, dropping his bag under the bumper.

"No," I said. "It's too full of totes and bags and stuff."

"And your cash register," he pointed to the small machine sitting on the SUV's carpeted floorboards.

I paused before saying, "It's empty. I always hide the money so if someone breaks in, they'll just get an ugly paperweight, but none of the cash." I grabbed a duffel bag, glanced at the hidden compartment that still looked secure, and locked the door again. "I sleep on this."

I pulled a folded air mattress and a hand pump from the bag. I opened the mattress on the ground, inserted the air pump nozzle, and began pumping. What was usually a mindless task now had me self-conscious. I must look ridiculous. Up and down, up and down. Do I bend my knees, or my back? Should I kneel so my ass isn't sticking out? Should I look at him or away from him? There was no way for me to look sexy or handsome while hunched over, furiously pumping.

I saw a flash of movement from the corner of my eye. Cass was shaking out a sheet that I'd had rolled up in the duffel bag. When the air mattress was finally full, Cass held out one corner of the fitted sheet and we made the bed. I tossed my pillow on last, then stood awkwardly beside the bed. I didn't want to lie down and look like I expected Cass to join me. I also didn't want to look like I *didn't* want him to join me.

Shut up, Callum, you're not a teenage girl.

Cass made the first move, as he had all day. He grabbed my hand and pulled me down on the bed beside him, so we were laying facing each other. He looked deep into my eyes and ran his fingers through my curls. A shiver ran down my spine. I wrapped my arms around him. We stayed that way for what could have been minutes or hours.

He kissed me gently. His lips were smooth. The few men I'd been with had dry lips and rough hands. But not Cass. His hands were soothing as they ran down my arms and up my back, under my shirt.

Desire coursed through my body, but I didn't push him faster. I wanted this to be slow and sweet, wanted to take our time and enjoy every inch of each other. He kissed me everywhere from my forehead to my ears to my neck. I couldn't help but moan. He pulled my shirt over my head, then continued kissing down my torso. When he slid his fingers inside the waistband of my kilt, I sucked in an anticipatory breath.

"Do you have a condom?" he asked with a husky voice.

"No, I don't." I covered my face with my hands in disbelief. "This has never happened to me before. I've never thought to bring one."

"Don't worry, I've got one." He kissed me, then crawled over to where he had dropped his bag.

I could hear him rifling through the bag but couldn't see him in the darkness of the canopy. It seemed to be taking a while for him to find it. I sat up and reached down to unlace my shoes.

"Do you always carry condoms with you?" I asked.

"Oh, I always come prepared," he whispered in my ear from behind me.

I felt a sudden sharp pain in my back. A split second later I felt the same pain in my head.

Rain and Fried Rice

I ended up in Hong Kong in July, the middle of the monsoon season. When I planned that leg of my trip, I didn't worry about it too much. I was going to spend most of my time in the restaurant anyway. Besides, I love rain and thunderstorms! Since childhood, I have loved watching the lightning cut the sky and feeling the thunder rumble through the house. But even I got tired of the rain after a month of no respite.

One thing I love about Chinese cuisine is that I can order the same food at ten different restaurants and get ten different—but equally amazing—meals. In Chinese culture, making a recipe one's own is not only accepted, but encouraged. It's how the culture has created such unique flavors and variations on classic recipes.

This is most evident with the Chinese staple of fried rice. Even with very few ingredients, this dish can vary wildly from place to place. My favorite fried rice was from a restaurant called The Horizon.

The owner, Mother Chen, took a liking to me after I praised her food. On my second visit, she started calling me by name, something I didn't see her do with any of the other patrons. She made it very clear that she wanted me to marry her son, Shang. She forced him to come out and tell me anything I wanted to know about her recipes—except for her fried rice.

One day, when the rain had lightened to a furious drizzle, she chased us out of the restaurant with a waving towel. By some miracle, the rain stopped the moment we stepped out of The Horizon. I couldn't help but dance in the puddles, much to Shang's delight. We walked and talked for most of the afternoon, solidifying a wonderful friendship.

When we returned to the restaurant, Mother Chen looked at us like she was expecting wedding bells. She was disappointed when Shang told her we had decided to stay friends. Her last-ditch effort was to offer me her fried rice recipe as a wedding present. I was honored that she was so excited to have me in the family, but we had to let her down gently one more time.

On my last day in Hong Kong, she did decide to give me the recipe after all. And an open invitation to come back whenever I wanted and marry Shang. Here's her recipe for her scrumptious fried rice.

Mother Chen's Fried Rice

PREP TIME: 15 mins
TOTAL TIME: 25 mins

COOK TIME: 10 mins
SERVINGS: 4-6 servings

INGREDIENTS

- 4 eggs, whisked
- 3 cups rice of choice, cooked and cooled
- 2 tablespoons sesame oil
- 1 white onion, chopped
- 2-3 tablespoons oyster sauce (can substitute soy sauce)
- 2 tablespoons green onions, chopped

INSTRUCTIONS

- Heat a large wok or skillet to medium-high heat.
- Add whisked eggs, seasoned as desired, and cook until firm and fluffy.
- Remove eggs to separate bowl and clean pan.
- Heat oil in pan.
- Add rice, sesame oil, onion, oyster sauce, and green onions.
- Stir and fry rice until warm.
- Add egg and stir to break up egg.
- Variations: peas, carrots, and meat of choice can be added during sauté.

Chapter 7

Iwas pulled from sleep by a delicious smell. *Cinnamon and syrup*, I thought. I opened one eye to see a plate heaped with fresh French Toast, dripping with syrup, and sprinkled with powdered sugar. Harper held the hot plate with a mitted hand—and nothing else.

"I made you 'I'm sorry for canceling date night' breakfast," she told me. "Are you hungry?"

"For you or for breakfast?"

"You can have both if you want," she said, licking her lips seductively.

"Breakfast first."

I grabbed the plate from Harper. She looked at me incredulously. I set the plate on my bedside table and pulled her on top of me. "I'm just kidding, my love. You know you are my favorite breakfast, snack, and dinner."

She rolled her eyes but let me kiss her neck and wrap my arms around her.

Between kisses I asked, "Can I sprinkle you with powdered sugar, though?"

* * * *

"Oh, good, it's still hot," I told her, pulling the plate of French toast onto my lap.

"It's only been three minutes," she teased.

"It was a strong five minutes, and you know it!" I threw the oven mitt at her.

"And it was the best sex of my life," she said with flat enthusiasm. "Seriously, though, I'm sorry about last night."

"It's fine," I mumbled through French toast.

"No, it's not. I hate that my unreliable sous chef cost us our date night. I want to get rid of him."

"Why don't you?"

"The boss won't let me," she pouted.

"You *are* the boss," I reminded her. "It's your restaurant. Your name is on the menu."

"Ugh, don't remind me!" She threw herself dramatically across the bed. "The problem is that when he *does* show up, he's the best sous chef I've ever had. I don't know what to do."

I patted her knee comfortingly. "I'm sure you'll figure it out."

She covered her face with a pillow and groaned into it. Then she peeked out from underneath and asked, "What did you do last night?"

"The usual," I said, mopping up the syrup with the last bite of French toast. "I did my nails, waxed my legs, and took a long bubble bath."

She hit me with the pillow. "Smart ass."

"I had a beer, watched a boxing match, and scratched myself in inappropriate places."

"You really know how to turn a lady on." She winked.

I laughed and walked my fingers up her leg from her knee to her thigh. When I was almost at her lady parts, she slapped my hand away.

"How did last night go? Did everyone else show up?" I asked.

"We killed it, honestly. It was a full crew, everything was prepped correctly, and no one complained about the food."

"That's great! I'm so proud of you."

She changed the subject. "What's on your agenda for the day?"

"Other than hoping I don't get called in to work? I'm not sure."

"Well, since you don't have anything super important…." She crawled across the bed to her nightstand and pulled a stack of papers from a drawer. "I want you to read these."

"Ooh, more recipes," I said. "Where in the world are we off to this time?"

"China, Poland, and Australia." She looked sheepish. "I still think I'm wasting my time writing these. I don't think anyone reads the introductions anyways, but all cookbooks by the celebrity chefs have them."

"I think the people that know you and love you and your cooking are going to enjoy all your stories. I know I've loved all of them."

"All of them?"

"Yes, Harper, *all* of them."

She gave me an appreciative kiss and then padded naked toward the en suite bathroom to shower. As much as I wanted to join her, I was too ashamed of myself. I had just lied to Harper. Again. When I said *I loved all of them*, I meant all of the ones I'd read. Not that I'd read all that she'd given me. And I had purposely misled her.

When I joined the Omaha PD, I refused to fill the stereotype of the officer that shut down his emotions and lost his sense of humor. When I met Harper, I promised myself that I wasn't going to be that cop that put my job in front of my marriage. When we got married, I vowed I would never act like my career was more important than Harper's.

Overall, I had supported her as much as possible. I'd tasted new dishes even if they contained ingredients I didn't like. I had even worked as a waiter and washed dishes at the restaurant. But reading the never-ending intros was more than I was able to juggle with my caseload. It just seemed that every time she gave me one, I had something big happen with a case at work. But I knew that wasn't a legitimate excuse; it was a cop-out.

I decided to spend all day reading the intros. That way, there would be no more lying or misleading Harper. Maybe this afternoon, when the guilt of being a lousy husband subsided, I would ask Harper for more of the dessert she gave me after her luncheon. Hopefully, we can share several helpings of dessert.

I jumped out of bed and put on my most comfortable shorts. I grabbed the new intros from the bed, poured myself a glass of orange juice in the kitchen, and headed for my favorite recliner. No sooner had I sunk into the recliner's thick cushions did the *Imperial March* scream from my cell phone. Chief Probst.

"Falco," I answered.

"Get down here, Falco," Chief Probst ordered. "We've got a body. It's getting hot fast, and you need to look at it so we can get it out of here."

"Where is *here*?"

"Omaha Park."

"Isn't there a renaissance fair there this weekend?"

"Midwestern Scottish-Irish Festival," he grunted.

"Geez, don't tell me this guy got stabbed with some archaic weapon."

"Nope, butcher knife. Get down here." *Click.*

I dragged my feet as I went back to the bedroom to change into my dress clothes. I opened the drawer of my bedside table and stared into it. A stack of at least ten intros was already sitting there, bright white paper glaring up at me. I added the three new intros to the pile, and slid the drawer shut before the guilt became too much.

In the kitchen, Harper was sitting at the large island working on her computer. I saw a Word document titled "Southern Comfort," and I realized that she was working on another recipe intro. Guilt twisted my stomach at the thought of adding it to my pile. She held out a travel mug filled with iced coffee.

"I heard the *Imperial March*," she said, "I know you have to go."

"I'd rather stay home with you," I said.

"I know you would, but the citizens of Omaha need you."

"What are you going to do today since you'll have the whole place to yourself?"

"Probably have a beer, watch a boxing match, and scratch myself in inappropriate places."

I laughed. "You are my perfect woman. Don't let anyone tell you any different."

"Stay safe," she said, kissing me goodbye. "Get the bad guy."

＊ ＊ ＊ ＊

"How in the hell did a butcher knife get here?" I asked. "Like, who brings a butcher knife into a festival? Or did he get it from a vendor? Or one of the food trucks?"

"I had uniformed officers talk to the vendors," Sophia said. "None of them claim to have any missing knives. There is one vendor selling knives, but he doesn't have anything close to this, just pocket knives and hunting knives. It's looks like our guy brought it in with him."

"So, this is premeditated?" I asked.

"Seems like it," Sophia confirmed.

We looked down at the body, lying neatly on a now-deflated air mattress. He could've been sleeping, one hand thrown over his eyes to shield them from the sun. Could have, if it weren't for the 10" butcher knife sticking out of his chest.

"Wowie, look what we have here?" Cathy called from the victim's SUV. She was waving a vinyl bank bag. It looked like it was stuffed full. "There's a whole lot of dough in here."

I glanced at the register sitting on some totes in the back.

"Why is his cash not in the register?" I asked.

"It was hidden," Cathy said.

67

I looked where Cathy was pointing. Just inside the rear door, there was a small panel removed from the plastic trim. I recognized it as the cover for the fuse panel. I had never considered using it as a hiding spot, but our victim had.

"Keep the cash hidden separate from the register," Cathy stated. "That way if someone breaks in, they'll take the register, but you don't lose any money. Makes sense to me."

"That confirms that this wasn't a robbery," I said. "The register is still here, and it doesn't look like any of the totes have been taken. All the tables and shelves look organized; not like they had been ransacked or had things removed."

Sophia glanced at the tables. "You're right."

"I love it when you say that," I teased.

Before she could smack me, a uniformed officer popped his head inside the tent. "Detectives, two witnesses want to speak to you."

I held the flap of the canopy for Sophia, then followed her out into the already sweltering heat. The officer took us to the blue canopy next to the victim's booth, where I could see tables and racks filled with knitted and crocheted items. An elderly couple stood huddled together. I could tell by the look on the man's face that he was going to be difficult to interview. He would talk over his wife the whole time. Most likely, he would only address me, ignoring Sophia completely. Eventually, he would try to get me to side with him as a man, which I wouldn't do. I decided to focus on the wife as much as I could.

"I'm Detective Leoni, this is Detective Falco," Sophia introduced us. "You are?"

"I'm Bernard Finnigan, and this is my wife, Laurel," said the old man. "I'm the one that found Callum this morning."

"I'm sorry you had to see that," Sophia said. "Can you tell us what happened this morning?"

"Why, yes, dear," Laurel said, her voice soft and slightly shaky. "We got here this morning around 7. We like to be here early to go through our inventory."

Right on cue, Bernard interrupted her. "No, it wasn't 7, it was 6:50 at the latest."

"Are you sure, honey?" Laurel asked. "I remember hearing the weather report on the radio before we pulled into the parking lot and that didn't come on until 6:50."

68

"I told you they were early! I pointed at the clock on the dash, and it said 6:45."

"That's when we turned off the road, but it took ten minutes or so to get across the grounds and park the car behind the booth," Laurel replied.

"It didn't take ten minutes," Bernard argued.

Sophia spoke over the squabble. "So, you were here around 7," she said loudly. "That's close enough for—"

"No, we need the right time," Bernard interrupted again. He glared at Sophia and spat, "If we tell you the wrong time, it'll mess up your whole investigation, or you'll think we're the murderers."

Normally, the thought of this frail couple wielding a large knife would have made me chuckle, but I was too focused on Mr. Finnigan's dis-respect toward Sophia. I knew not to address the issue directly, that Sophia would put Bernard in his place if she wanted to. But she would be furious with me if I went to her rescue like she was incapable of defending herself. Instead, I turned away from Bernard, focusing all my attention on Laurel.

"You're doing just fine, Mrs. Finnigan. What happened after you got to your booth?"

"We got everything ready for the day," Laurel said. "You see, we have everything organized in totes, so I know what we've sold, and I've got a clipboard where—"

"They don't want to hear about that, Laurel," Bernard snapped. "They want to know about the *crime*."

"Yes, please," Sophia said. "What happened just before you found the body?"

"It was almost 8:00," Bernard said. "I noticed Callum hadn't rolled up the flaps on his canopy yet. But we knew he was here."

"Callum sleeps on an air mattress in there," Laurel explained, tipping her head toward his plaid canopy. "He doesn't want to spend money on hotels, so he stays here. He also keeps an eye on the booths."

"There's no security here at night, so sometimes stuff gets taken." Bernard leaned toward me, conspiratorially. "I'm sure you get plenty of calls to these types of events. People don't want to work anymore. You know how they steal instead of getting a job. Back in my day—"

"Is he usually punctual?" I asked, cutting Bernard off.

"Oh, yes, he's always the first one open in the morning," Laurel said. "We thought he was just in the bathroom getting ready."

69

"It takes a long time to fix his curly hair," Bernard scoffed. "He should just cut it; he's not a hippie—"

"What happened next?" I cut in.

"I decided to help him," Bernard said, puffing his chest like he had saved a life. "I'm used to kids these days being useless without someone to help them."

"How were you going to help him?" I asked.

"I was going to get his canopy sides rolled up so that it was ready to go when he got back," Bernard explained. "I had the first flap up before I saw Callum's body."

"What did you do next?"

"Well, I could tell he was dead." He gave me a pointed look. "We watch CSI, so I know what a dead body looks like."

"I see...." I wasn't sure how to respond. He didn't seem to notice that I wasn't impressed; he just kept talking.

"So, I put the flap back down so no one would disturb the crime scene, then called the police."

"And no one else went inside until the cops got here?" Sophia asked.

"Oh, heaven's no," Laurel said proudly. "We stood outside and told people he was sick and to not bother him."

"It sounds like you knew Callum pretty well," I pointed out.

"Only professionally," Bernard said. "We see him every year at several of the events and craft shows around Omaha."

"Yet you know him well enough to know his sleep set up?" I pushed.

"Don't overthink it, dear," Laurel's shaky voice reassured me. "These events can get boring sometimes, so we like talking to our neighbors. We've met some swell young people that way. And it makes the time go by faster."

"You didn't know anything else personal about him?" I asked.

"Didn't know and didn't want to know," Bernard sneered. "These kids today are too touchy. You can't ask them anything or give your opinion about anything. You never know what'll set them off."

Bernard took a few steps away from us. I could tell he was done with our conversation but also wanted to stay close enough to add his two cents whenever he wanted. Laurel stayed behind, wringing her hands, like she was bursting to tell us something else.

"Mrs. Finnigan, what else would you like us to know?" I asked softly.

"I didn't tell Bernard because he can be rather...." she searched for the right word, "Old-fashioned."

I thought there were stronger words closer to the truth, but that was just my personal opinion. I nodded for her to continue.

"I knew Callum was a gay," she chirped. "Not that I have anything against the gays. I've just never known a gay before. It was quite exciting to know that I had a friend that was a gay."

Laurel looked proud of herself for being so inclusive, even if she was being discriminatory.

"How did you know Callum was homosexual?" I asked.

"Earlier this summer at the county fair, he had a booth down the way from us," she explained. "Several days, a nice young man brought him food and sat with him."

"And you're sure that it was someone he was involved with? Not a relative or friend?"

She gave me a motherly look like I was a child that needed to learn the ways of the world. "You don't look at a relative the way he looked at that young man."

"I'll take your word for it," I said. "Have you noticed anyone hanging around the last few days?"

"Oh, yes, there was a nice young man here yesterday helping him," she said. "I heard him say he was Callum's brother, but that was just part of his act."

Sophia perked up. "What act?"

Bernard couldn't resist the urge to shout, "It wasn't an act, it was a sham!"

"What do you mean?" Sophia asked.

"Callum uses a Scottish accent at this festival," Bernard said, stomping back to us. "He speaks perfect American at any other event we've seen him at, but when we get here, he's suddenly fresh off the boat from Scotland."

"He's just having fun, Bernard," Laurel scolded. "Let the young man be."

Bernard walked off again, out the back of his canopy, mumbling about respect. Unsurprisingly, Bernard couldn't handle being told off by his wife. I was proud of her, though.

Laurel waved a hand dismissively over her shoulder. "Don't mind him," she said, "He's just an opinionated old fart."

I smiled at her comment, but Sophia was all business. "What can you tell us about the man you saw helping Callum yesterday?"

"He was a small fella. A little on the shorter side and scrawny. He needs more meat and potatoes in his diet," she instructed. "And he wore all black, despite the heat. I don't know how he could stand it."

"Anything else distinct about him? Hair color, scars, anything like that?"

"No, I'm sorry. He had short hair but was wearing a ball cap, so I don't know what color it was. And he was straight as a board no matter how you looked at him." She drew her hands down in front of her like blades, emphasizing *straight*. "I guess not completely straight, since he was a gay, but you know what I mean."

"How did you know he was gay?" I was careful not to copy her and say *a* gay.

"I saw him and Callum at the Calling. They were *holding hands*." She whispered the last two words like they were scandalous to delicate ears.

"Thank you for your help, Mrs. Finnigan. Please, let us know if you think of anything else." I handed her my business card.

We were almost to Callum's canopy when Sophia suddenly turned around and asked Laurel, "Any chance you heard him say his name?"

"Hmmm," she put her fingers on her chin thoughtfully. "Oh, yes, his name was Cass."

"Thank you, Laurel," Sophia said. She turned to me. "Isn't Cass the name Jason the bartender gave us?"

"Yeah, it is. But she seems pretty sharp for her age. What are the chances she heard the name wrong?"

"I don't know." She changed the subject. "We've got plenty of other things to work on today, though."

The rest of Sunday was a blur of activity at the Midwest Scottish-Irish Festival. Sophia and I split up to talk to the event organizers, security guards, and any vendors or guests that wanted to speak with us. By the time we met up at 8:30 pm, we were both exhausted. We sat in my car with the air conditioner running full blast to review everything we'd discovered, which wasn't much.

Sophia held up a flash drive. "I've got the raw pictures from the event's photographer, Bryony. She warned us that not all the pictures would be perfect, but there are thousands here from the whole event, including last night."

"Wow," I said, impressed. "She just handed it over to you? No grief about getting a warrant or the rights of the strangers in the photos?"

"Nope, none of the usual hoops to jump through. Bryony said she wanted to help any way she could. She did ask that we not tell anyone where we got the pictures, though. She didn't want us to release a blurry picture with her name attached; people might think that was the final product."

"Sounds reasonable enough." I flipped open my notebook. "I got a lead from one of the food trucks that he had eaten at the shepherd's pie place. I checked with the owner, and he remembered seeing our vic but said he was alone. He was sure about it because he didn't ask for an extra fork and, apparently, that's hard proof that he wasn't sharing his meal with anyone."

"He's got a point," Sophia agreed. "Who would share a fork with a perfect stranger?"

"Don't ask me. I won't even share a fork with Harper."

"Any other good witnesses to the crime or possible suspects?"

"Nothing," I said, shaking my head. "They either didn't see anything and were just being nosy, or they think they saw everything but were useless."

"So far, we have the victim's name and the murder weapon. We don't think it was a robbery, but we also don't think he was with anyone last night."

"Right," I said absentmindedly.

"Uh oh, you've got that look in your eye," Sophia warned. "What are you thinking?"

"I think this is related to the Barn Sour murder," I said.

"Why? There's nothing similar."

"There's the description of the suspect and the name," I reminded her.

"A short, skinny guy with short hair? Come on, Dawson, you know that describes hundreds of men in Omaha. That's excluding the fact that both murders occurred where there was high traffic of visitors from outside the city," Sophia pointed out. "Sure, Cass isn't the most common name, but it could be a shortened name or a nickname. Or Mrs. Finnigan could've misheard the name."

I blew out a sigh, not wanting to admit that she may be right. "I just have a gut feeling on this one, Sophia. These two are linked somehow. I just know it."

"You know we can't take a gut feeling to court. We have to work this like any other case."

"Ugh, I hate it when you're all *wise*," I teased her, receiving a punch to the arm.

"What else can we do tonight?"

"I think we can call it a night. The crowd is gone, and all the vendors are leaving. I don't think we'll figure anything else out until we get the autopsy results and can look at those pictures. Let's meet back at the station tomorrow morning and make a game plan."

Sophia climbed out of my car. She leaned down and spoke to me through the window. "Have you read any more of Harper's intros?"

"I read the one about our honeymoon. And it made me feel worse for not helping," I admitted.

"Enough that you're going to bust your ass to get them all done?" she asked sternly.

"Yes, I'll get them done," I said. "I'll bring some to work tomorrow and read as many as I can."

"That sounds like something a good husband would do. Harper deserves one of those." She gave me a pointed look, then said, "See you in the morning."

Too Outback for Me

I didn't spend much time in Australia, mostly because of timing and logistics. Also, as beautiful as the country is, I couldn't overcome my slightly irrational fear of being eaten by the plethora of scary animals there: crocodiles, sharks, and snakes.

While there, I lived with and learned from a beautiful and brilliant young Aboriginal woman named Jannali. She was the granddaughter of her tribe's chief and served as an educator and ambassador for her tribe. She traveled the world advocating for Aboriginals and helping keep their culture alive.

I spent several weeks with her in her ancestral village, learning how her people hunted and foraged for food and how their cooking had evolved over the centuries. Seeing what they could create without modern technology and equipment was impressive.

As adventurous as I am with trying new foods, I had to really open my mind to some of the typical meat choices: possums, a rodent in the US, was quite juicy; echidnas tasted like chicken; crocodile was tough when cooked fresh but tasted better when dehydrated into jerky. Though I hated to seem rude, I couldn't bring myself to eat snakes or lizards. Luckily, Jannali was sympathetic to my limitations. She told me most people didn't make it that far into the menu, so she was proud of me anyways. She treated me to a more modern Australian staple, the Carpetbag Steak.

Jannali also showed me the hidden beauties of her homeland. We sat by a bonfire most evenings, looking at the stars and listening to tribe elders tell stories from their youth. During the day, she showed me how to spot and avoid all the animals I was worried would make me a meal.

I learned so many good recipes I would love to share with the world, but most of the meat they used isn't available at the local grocery store. (Check out *Food from the Earth* for Aboriginal recipes) Instead, I'll share the recipe for the carpet bag steak I enjoyed with Jannali. Don't let the name fool you, this dish is *waratah*—beautiful.

Australian Carpetbag Steak with Garlic Butter

PREP TIME: 20 min
TOTAL TIME: 40 min

COOK TIME: 20 min
SERVINGS: 4 servings

INGREDIENTS FOR STEAK

- 4 sirloin steaks
- 12 oysters, shucked and cleaned
- 2 tablespoons olive oil

GARLIC BUTTER

- ¾ cup unsalted butter, softened
- 7 cloves garlic, crushed
- ½ cup parsley leaves
- ½ cup lemon juice, freshly squeezed

INSTRUCTIONS

- Let steaks come to room temperature, seasoning as desired. Preheat oven to 350°.
- Make garlic butter in large mixing bowl, whisk all ingredients together until blended smooth.
- Cut slit in each steak to create a pocket.
- Fill with 3 oysters and desired portion of garlic butter. Pinch closed and secure with toothpicks.
- Heat oil in oven safe frying pan or skillet.
- Cook steaks until brown, approximately 4-5 minutes.
- Put pan and steaks in preheated oven and cook to desired temperature, approximately 8-10 minutes for medium.
- Remove from oven and let rest for 5 minutes. Serve hot.

Chapter 8

The ID found in Callum's SUV had his permanent address listed as Boston. Monday morning, Sophia sent a request for DMV and criminal records. By noon, she had two emails with small files attached.

"Callum McIntyre, age 27," Sophia read aloud to me. "No criminal history, no warrants, not so much as a speeding ticket on his record. Our guy is squeaky clean."

"Any jilted ex's that may have come after him?"

"I doubt it. Callum's never taken out a restraining order, been a victim of domestic violence, or any other indicators that he may have a bad ex-boyfriend. And he's never had anything similar charged against him that would make it seem like *he* was the bad ex-boyfriend."

His registered address was also his mother's address. It's not uncommon for young adults to keep their parent's address on record until they've settled down. Especially since Callum spent most of his time on the road. I called the number listed for Norma McIntyre, putting the call on speaker so Sophia could hear.

"Hello?" answered a deep male voice.

"Hello, this is Detective Dawson Falco calling from the Omaha Police Department. Is there a Norma McIntyre available?"

"What's this about?" the man asked, his voice hard.

"I'm calling in regard to Mrs. McIntyre's son, Callum. Can we speak with her?"

"I'm Callum's older brother, Duncan. My mother has dementia, so you can talk to me."

"Mr. McIntyre—"

"Duncan," he corrected.

"Right, Duncan. I'm sorry to tell you this, but your brother has been murdered," I said.

"Sorry, I don't think I heard you right," Duncan said. "Did you just say my brother was murdered?"

"Yes, Duncan. He was found yesterday at the Midwestern Scottish-Irish Festival here in Omaha."

There was silence for a long moment. Sophia and I looked at each other, not sure if we dropped the call. My phone screen showed that the call was still connected.

"Duncan? Are you still there?"

"Y-yes, I'm here. I'm just—" and he burst into tears.

"Take your time, Duncan," Sophia said softly.

A few minutes later, his crying began to subside. "What happened?" he choked.

"His case is still under investigation, but it appears he was stabbed by someone he knew while he was working at the festival," I said.

"Do you know anyone who might want to hurt your brother?" Sophia asked gently.

"No, no one," Duncan said, his voice shaky. "I know it sounds cliché, but everyone liked Callum. No matter the crowd or what he was doing, he just fit in with everyone. He had a way of talking to people on their level without buying into their bullshit. He was the only one that could handle my *ist* uncles."

"Pardon, *ist* uncles?" I asked, not familiar with the term.

"Yeah, rac*ist*, sex*ist*, age*ist*. The ones that are too old to change their ways but too young to die soon so we don't have to deal with them. The uncles no one actually wants to invite to Thanksgiving but your grandma makes you."

"We've all had those uncles," Sophia assured him. "And those thoughts. How was Callum able to handle them so well?"

"He was like a chameleon," Duncan said. "He could talk the talk with a sleazy lawyer just as easily as he could a librarian. And everyone just believed him. I only caught on when he came to my office to sell insurance. I told him he would never get past my jackass boss. But when I walked by his office, I heard them talking about the debt ceiling—which I know for a fact Callum knows nothing about. But Callum had
        had him eating out of the palm of his hand."

"We were told by witnesses that Callum was using a Scottish accent at the festival. Does that seem like something Callum would do?" I asked.

"It does." Duncan let out a pained laugh. "When we were kids, our dad bailed on us and mom worked a lot, so we were basically raised by the TV. We watched movies and he would pick up the accents. Braveheart and Bond were his favorites. I've seen him use the Bond voice to pick up girls."

I glanced at Sophia. This was our chance to find out if Callum was indeed gay or if that was another part of his act. I wanted to tread carefully in case Callum hadn't come out to his family. I didn't want to affect their view of him.

"Was your brother involved with any women that you were aware of?" I asked.

"He was gay," Duncan said, "He came out four or five years ago."

I breathed a sigh of relief. "Were there any boyfriends, then?"

"I doubt it. He was so busy with his job. He worked so hard. Mom is in a dementia care facility now. Her insurance doesn't cover much of it, so Callum's been taking care of it. I pitch in when I can, but I've got my own family to take care of."

"I understand, Mr. McIntyre. Your brother sounds like he was a good man," I said, trying to provide some comfort.

"He was," he choked out. "Do you have any other questions for me? I need to start calling my family and making funeral arrangements."

"No, that's all for now. Thank you, Mr. McIntyre. We will keep you notified of any developments in the case."

After he disconnected, Sophia and I sat for a few minutes, thinking to ourselves.

"That never gets any easier, does it?" Sophia asked.

"No, it doesn't."

* * * *

That afternoon, Sophia and I put on masks and gloves before pushing through the door to the autopsy room at the coroner's office. I hated this room more than anywhere else in the world. It was cold and sterile, and there was always a faint chemical smell, probably coming from the weird things in jars on shelves along the walls. I had to pretend there weren't dead bodies in the refrigerated drawers along the far wall. Seeing bodies at a crime scene didn't faze me, but the thought of bodies lying there waiting to be cut open was unsettling to me.

There were two stainless steel tables in the middle of the room. Callum McIntyre was on one of the tables, a sheet covering his legs and torso. Cathy was supposed to be here by now, but Callum was the only other person in the room.

"Cathy," I called out. "Are you here?"

She obviously wasn't. The room was square with no connecting rooms and no doors besides the one we just came through. There was nowhere for her to hide—except the refrigerator drawers.

"I swear to god," I whispered tensely to Sophia, "If she pops out of one of those drawers, I'm going to push her back in and lock her in it."

"You know that wouldn't bother her," Sophia whispered back. "She loves this place."

"It would be a little cold, don't you think?" Cathy said behind me, appearing out of nowhere.

I jumped and let out a screech. "Jesus, Cathy, why do you do that to me? You know I hate this place!"

"You're such a wimp," Cathy said. Then she looked at Sophia. "How do you put up with this guy?"

"I drink," Sophia said simply.

Cathy nodded her support before plucking a clipboard off the hook at the end of the table. "All right, scaredy cat, what would you like to know about this young man?"

"Cause of death?" I asked.

"A big ol' knife whacked him," she replied. "The one to the back of the head killed him. The rest were just for fun."

"For fun?"

"That's right, fun. They didn't cause any mortal damage but would've hurt more than a tickle. Your suspect did it just because he could." She tipped the body toward herself so we could see his back. She pointed to one of the wounds, directly into the spine. "This was the first blow, probably an attempt to paralyze him."

"And the rest?"

"Like I said, these were just to inflict pain until he died."

"Anything else we can learn from the body?" Sophia asked.

"Sadly, no. The vic has no tattoos that might indicate gang affiliation. He didn't smoke and his liver was perfect. The toxicology report shows no drugs in his system, prescribed or otherwise. His blood alcohol level was 0.02%, so he probably had one drink during the day. Based on the stomach contents, he'd had some whiskey.

"What else was in his stomach?" I asked.

"Some sort of casserole," Cathy said. "There was meat, veggies, and mashed potatoes."

"That sounds like shepherd's pie," I said.

Cathy raised an eyebrow. "How did you come up with that so quickly?"

"I talked to a vendor that claimed to have sold our vic a shepherd's pie," I said. "And it's one of Harper's favorite dishes. She used to make it all the time when we first got together."

"I bet you won't want to eat it now," Cathy said.

"You know how good Harper's cooking is, so you tell me," I teased. "Did you find anything to link this murder to our Barn Sour murder?"

"Not that I noticed," she said. "The victims couldn't be any more different. Should there have been a link?"

I thought before answering. "Maybe not. The only similarity we have is the description of the possible suspect and the fact that they weren't robberies. And the weapons."

"The Barn Sour girl was killed with blunt force trauma from a frying pan," Cathy said. "This guy was chopped with a knife. How are those weapons similar?"

"They are both kitchen utensils," I said.

"Right," Cathy said, skeptically, "But that's not really a connection. That would be like saying all gunshot deaths are related because they involve a bullet."

I glared at her. "That's not the same thing. There's just something about those two specific weapons. Maybe it's because they are so random and weird? I don't know, but I can't help thinking they are tied together."

"The frying pan seems more like a weapon of opportunity," Sophia argued. "It's not a weapon we've ever seen used before."

"I don't think you have enough to go on, Falco," Cathy said.

"Come on, Dawson," Sophia tugged at my sleeve. "This room is getting to you. Let's go to the war room and see what else we have."

* * * *

In the war room, Sophia and I pulled a table away from the wall and placed it beside Grace's evidence table. We began grabbing Callum's paperwork and evidence from our desks and arranging it on the table. The murder weapon was in an evidence bag, but the lab couldn't lift any prints. We had a dozen pages of fingerprints collected from Callum's booth. With the number of strangers that visited his booth during the events, it was unlikely to be helpful. The thumb drive from the official photographer sat next to two laptops.

Sophia inserted the flash drive into her laptop first. A warning popped up: **DRIVE PHOTO: 10,684 files detected. Would you like to continue downloading?**

We looked at each other, mouths agape. Over 10,000 pictures? That's several hundred pictures per hour during the four days of the festival. This was going to take us ages to go through, even with the two of us.

"Let's get to it," I said.

I downloaded the files onto the second laptop so we could split the work. Based on the eyewitness statements, we knew our suspect was hanging around the festival throughout the afternoon and evening, so we focused on Saturday's pictures. We each made separate folders labeled REVIEW for photos that needed another look, ones that could show our victim or a possible suspect. Sophia started with the morning pictures and worked forward; I started with the evening pictures and worked my way backward.

"I've got something!" I yelled after an hour. "Check this out!"

I was looking at a series of pictures from the Calling. There, in the front row, sat Callum. He was sharing a plate of food with someone. They were sitting angled toward each other, so the pictures showed Callum's face, but only the back of the suspect. I scrolled rapidly through the shots, but there weren't any better pictures.

Sophia turned my laptop so she could see better. "It looks like Finnigans' description was correct. He's about 5'7", skinny, and has short hair. And he's wearing all black."

"And you know who else matches that description?"

She cut her eyes quickly at me. "It may match Grace's killer, but that doesn't mean the murders are connected."

"Come on, Sophia, you can't deny that this is more than a coin-cidence! Same description, same name. They even both wore all black."

She sighed. "I'm still not convinced. Now that you know what to look for, hopefully you'll be able to find a better picture. One with his face would be great."

"*Then* will you believe me?"

"Show me the evidence," Sophia said, turning back to her laptop.

It only took another hour for me to finish going through the Calling photos. I moved one hundred or so pictures to my REVIEW folder. They all showed Callum and some part of the suspect, but none of them showed our suspect's face. I continued working my way backward through Saturday, hoping to track either Callum or the suspect through the day.

Three long hours later, my eyes couldn't focus anymore. At any other festival, it would've been easy to find Callum's bright red hair in the crowd. That wasn't the case at a festival specific to a heritage known for redheads. There were hundreds of red heads at the festival. Multiple times I thought I saw Callum, but it turned out to be another young man with curly red hair.

Finding possible suspects was difficult, too. Not only were skinny men of average build prevalent, but I knew I had to look at physical similarities and not rely on the all-black outfit. He might have changed outfits throughout the day. So far, though, I haven't seen him anywhere besides the Calling.

I threw a pen across the room. "Why can't I find this guy again!" I yelled. "He was right there. How did he manage to keep his face hidden in every shot? There's no way he could have known where the photographer was all day. There has to be a picture of his face somewhere, right?"

Sophia didn't speak. She kept clicking rapidly through a collection of still-shots from the Calling. **click click, click click** It was driving me crazy.

"Could you stop?" I barked. "I can't handle the clicking."

"I'm not trying to annoy you," she hissed. "I think I found something."

"What?"

"Look here," she pointed at the screen. "The photographer, Bryony, was taking pictures of the grandstand before the last show on Saturday night. She managed to get pictures of Callum and our suspect walking away from her to their seats. She had the camera switched to take rapid shots, which takes ten pictures per second."

"Why is that important?"

"If I click through them fast enough, it makes a stop-gap movie." She tilted her head as she continued staring at the computer screen. "Sort of."

"How is that going to help us?" I asked testily.

"Because I can see him walk. I think he—"

"We saw him walk in the videos from Barn Sour," I pointed out. "It didn't tell us anything useful, though. No limp, no sign of a disability, nothing."

She finally stopped looking at the computer. She seemed a little annoyed with me. "That footage was from a downward angle, and his cowboy hat blocked most of his body. This angle shows him at ground level from directly behind."

"What does that tell us about him?"

"That's just the thing. I don't think it's him."

"Him who?"

"I don't think it's a *him*. I think it's a *her*."

I laughed. She was really grasping at straws now. She made fun of me for thinking the cases were connected, but now she's telling me we have the whole gender wrong. It was impossible. She turned back to the computer and clicked through the pictures. I looked over her shoulder, but I didn't see what she saw.

"It's just a regular guy's walk," I said.

"No, it isn't. Men walk from their knees; women walk from their hips. That's why we shake our asses when we walk." She pointed at the screen. "This person is moving their hips more than Callum."

She clicked through the pictures again, pointing at the backside of our suspect. I glanced from him to Callum and back again.

"Everyone walks differently," I argued. "Lots of things affect how a person walks: leg size and length, shoe type, injuries—"

"Yes, thank you for mansplaining walking to me," Sophia snapped. "I'm aware of how walking works."

I held my hands up in surrender, but I still wasn't convinced. Then again, I had never been an ass-man, so I'd never watched how butts or hips moved for either gender. As a whole, though, that body was definitely a man's.

"Look at that figure, though, Sophia. If that's a woman, she has no curves. That *has* to be a dude. Women aren't that—" I made the same chopping motion that Laurel Finnigan had, "—straight."

"That's very sexist of you," Sophia admonished. "Plenty of small women can pull off a male disguise."

"Name one," I challenged.

"Hillary Swank, Cate Blanchett, Glen Close, just to name a few off the top of my head."

"Those are celebrities," I argued. "They have makeup and prosthetics. That hardly counts."

"What about Harper?" she pointed out. "Harper doesn't have a lot of curves. For all we know, that's her in the pictures."

We immediately started laughing.

"Fine, fine, I get your point," I admitted. "I'm still not going to stop looking at men, but I won't rule out the *possibility* that that could be a woman."

"And I won't rule out the *possibility* that maybe Grace and Callum's cases are connected." Sophia laughed again. "Could you imagine Harper murdering someone? She's the nicest person I've ever met; there's no way she could pull off a murder."

"If I tell her that you thought she was our murderer, she'll never make you another meal again."

"You wouldn't!" Sophia gasped.

"Oh, I would," I teased.

Dancing in the South

Like most women, I spent my teenage and college years feeling pressured by society to look a certain way. As an adopted child, I had no way to know what role genetics would play in my body. So, I had to err on the side of caution, and I missed out on some of the best foods in the world because of it. That's a hard pill for a chef to swallow. Before my last year of culinary school, I decided I'd had enough! To make up for lost time, I spent my summer internship in a place that doesn't count calories, that doesn't know the meaning of trans fats, and that shows comfort in all the best ways: the South. I went down to Southern Georgia to fill up on all the comfort foods I had deprived myself of: fried chicken, grits, fried green tomatoes, homemade buttermilk biscuits, and so much more.

While there, I met the young woman who was the epitome of a Southern Belle. Her name was Angel, and she was beautiful, polite, and funny. Did that girl ever love to dance! Her favorite dance to attend was not a debutante's ball but a hoedown. That's right, an honest-to-god flannel wearing, banjo plucking, dance move calling, hoedown.

The first time she invited me, I thought she was joking. I thought hoedowns were a Hollywood invention used to make Southerners look bad. I didn't know they were a real—and popular—activity. I agreed to go simply to say, "I tried it once, I didn't like it, I don't want to go again, no thank you." Except that none of those things ended up being true. I *loved* the hoedown. It took me some time to figure out the steps and keep up with the crowd, but I picked it up. Angel and I would dance and twirl for hours each weekend.

Though Angel and I weren't connected through the kitchen, she was still a very important person to me. She reminded me what it felt like to do things because I wanted to, without shame, and with an open heart and mind. So, I asked Angel what her favorite meal was. I wasn't surprised when she told me chicken fried steak, creamy gravy, collard greens, mashed potatoes, and a fresh-baked roll. All of it made from scratch, of course.

As a bonus, talking to her made me realize that I haven't been dancing in so many years! Since I know my husband loves this recipe, I'll have to use it as a bargaining tool to get him to take me swing dancing.

Chicken Fried Steak and Country Gravy

PREP TIME: 15 min
TOTAL TIME: 30 min

COOK TIME: 15 min
SERVINGS: 4 servings

INGREDIENTS FOR STEAK
- 1 pound cube steak
- ¾ cup milk
- 1 large egg
- ¾ cup flour
- 1½ teaspoons seasoning salt
- ½ teaspoon ground black pepper

COUNTRY GRAVY
- ¼ cup butter (or oil from cooking meat)
- ⅓ cup flour
- 2 cups whole milk

INSTRUCTIONS
- In one mixing bowl, whisk milk and egg. In a second bowl, mix flour, salt, and pepper.
- Coat each steak completely in flour, then milk, then flour, shaking off excess each time. (Let sit in fridge for 20 minutes for thicker breading)
- Heat oil in large skillet on medium heat. Fry each steak for 2 minutes on each side until golden brown. Remove and place on paper towel. (For extra crispy, let cool slightly, then refry)
- For gravy, heat clean saucepan on medium heat and add butter. Whisk in flour, stirring constantly for 2-3 minutes.
- Slowly whisk in milk, stirring constantly.
- Cook for 6-8 minutes, add salt and pepper to taste.
- Serve steak and gravy warm.

Chapter 9

I can't do it anymore," I complained to Sophia. "I can't read one more line!"

This morning, I was working on a new type of hell: tracking down distributors of our murder weapons. I had hoped that the brand of skillet and knife was so high-end and exclusive that there wouldn't be many places selling them. The fewer stores that sell them, the more likely it was that someone at the store would recognize our suspect. Best case scenario, we would get an ID, a name from a credit card, or a picture from a security camera. So far, though, hundreds of stores in Omaha and the surrounding towns carried one or both brands of our murder weapons.

"Quit being dramatic," Sophia scolded. "I think you're just hungry. Maybe you should eat something."

I suddenly thought of a way to kill two birds with one stone. "You are absolutely right, Sophia. Let's go."

"Where are we headed?" Sophia asked me.

"To get lunch," I said, "And to talk to an expert!"

"We're going to Harper's restaurant, aren't we?"

"Like I said, lunch and an expert."

It was past 1:30 when I pulled into the Old Market. I loved this part of downtown Omaha because it was a perfect blend of classic architecture and modern updates. The buildings were all red brick with tall narrow windows on the second story. Ivy vines and rose trellises covered large portions of the brick. Most of the roads were still cobble-stone. The lower levels of the buildings had all been converted into boutique stores or trendy restaurants with large front windows, and the second stories were renovated apartments. It was twelve square blocks of old-school beauty.

I was lucky enough to find parking in front of Clever Culinary, which was in the middle of the main block. I peered through the window to make sure the dining room was empty. There were a few tables with diners, but I was confident that Harper would be free for a consultation.

The dining room had 15 tables arranged in the middle of the floor. Red horseshoe booths lined both walls, and a bar stood at the far end, lights reflecting through liquor bottles. The wall was covered with artsy pictures of Harper's favorite dishes. My favorite was the plate of her specialty chicken wings, but I glanced at the picture of the shepherd's pie as I walked past. I admired the display of Harper's accomplishments, too.

We took a seat at the bar as Jean-Pierre bustled through the swinging door from the kitchen. When he saw us, he beamed with joy.

"Detective Falco, Detective Leoni! How *wonderful* to see you!"

"Please, Jean-Pierre, just Dawson and Sophia," I reminded him.

"I know, I know," he said, "You tell me that every time. But I just *can't* bring myself to call you that. You are fine officers of the law; you *deserve* to be referred to by your titles!"

"I appreciate that," Sophia said, "But I'm not just a cop. I'm also just a person who wants to be called Sophia."

He looked at her like she was crazy. "How about Detective *Sophia?*" he suggested.

"Deal," Sophia said.

"Now, Detective and Detective Sophia, what can I get for you?" he asked. "Can I start you off with a drink? A nice glass of *pinot grigio?* Or perhaps a chilled dessert wine to *cleanse* your pallet on this hot day?"

"Just a few beers, please," I said politely.

Jean-Pierre put his hands on his hips and stared at me. "Honestly, Detective, I don't know why your *brilliant* wife keeps you around. You have *no* taste for the finer things in life."

"I know why she keeps me around, Jean-Pierre. But it's not polite to discuss bedroom things in public."

He swatted me playfully with a towel. "Detective, you're such a *tease.*"

After he poured us two chilled glasses of beer, he flounced back into the kitchen to get Harper.

"He is one unique man," Sophia said.

"You don't know the half of it." I took a swig of my beer. When she quirked her eyebrow at me, I continued. "He's from a tiny town in Western Nebraska.

He came out to his family after high school, and it didn't go very well. So, he ran off to the big city! He only got as far as Omaha, but he seems happy here."

"His parents couldn't handle him being gay, but had no problem naming him *Jean-Pierre*?" She said it with a heavy French pronunciation.

"His real name is actually John Peter. But, new life, new name, I guess."

Sophia's nose wrinkled. "He's definitely more of a Jean-Pierre than a John Peter."

I nodded and raised my glass to her. She clanked hers to mine and said, "To Jean-Pierre."

Harper pushed through the kitchen door. "If you want me to get Jean-Pierre, he can cook you some of his famous bologna cups and peas." When Sophia and I both sneered in disgust, she said, "Don't knock it until you try it."

"Are there any other special treats two hardworking detectives can get for lunch?" I asked.

Harper looked at Sophia. "I'll make you anything you want, but who's the other hardworking detective?"

Sophia almost choked on her beer, and I gave Harper a shocked look. She high-fived Sophia, then gave me a wet kiss on the cheek.

"Give me ten minutes and I'll whip something up for you," she said before disappearing into the kitchen.

Jean-Pierre bustled back through the door. He busied himself putting away the bar's glassware. He wiped each glass with a towel before holding it to the light. When it was free of blemishes, he put it away. The whole time, he chatted away about the new man in his life, emphasizing words for dramatic effect.

"You know, Detectives, I think it's *about time* I found someone nice. I'm getting *too old* to fuss with men that don't know what they want. Or worse, *mama's boys*." He widened his eyes in horror at the thought.

"Jean-Pierre, how old are you?" I asked.

"Detective, one should never ask a lady or a *fabulous* man about their age," he chided. "But I'll tell you anyway. I'm *twenty-three*. Can you *believe* it? I don't look a *day* over twenty-one, but I'm as single as an old *maid*."

Sophia gave him a wry look. "I'm thirty and I haven't dated anyone in years. Does that make me an old maid."

"*Honey*, I didn't mean it like that. The rules are *different* for women," he patted her hand. "You'll find someone, sweetie."

Sophia didn't take kindly to people commenting about her relationship

90

status. Jean-Pierre knew this, so I worried that Sophia would jump across the bar and go after him. To save the situation, I cut in.

"By the way, Jean-Pierre, you've got to quit taking Harper away from me on our date nights. You know she can't tell you no, even if she has no problem telling *me* no."

"Detective, *what* are you talking about? It's been *months* since Harper's had to cancel date night."

"No, it was just last week. I was going to take her dancing at Barn Sour." When Sophia eyed me warily, I explained. "After you left dinner last week, Harper was mad that I had misled her on how many of her intros I'd read—"

"—You lied to her, you mean," Sophia cut in.

"I *misled* her," I clarified. "That night I read one about when she spent the summer in the South. She talked about going to hoe downs with a friend. The last line said she was going to withhold chicken fried steak until I took her dancing. I don't want that to happen, so Friday night I told her I was taking her to Barn Sour for date night."

"Aren't you just a *lesson* on romance," Jean-Pierre said sarcastically.

"Give me a break!" I said. "You know I do better than most men."

"That's not saying a lot," Sophia said under her breath.

Jean-Pierre winked at her dramatically. "Detective Sophia, you are a *gem*. Now, you sir," he pointed a wine glass at me, "must be confused. Harper *wasn't* here Saturday night."

"She told me the sous chef bailed again and she had to cover the kitchen."

"I don't think so," Jean-Pierre said. "Saturday, we served—"

"Who's ready for lunch?" Harper called, backing through the kitchen door, carrying two plates of food. "Chicken paninis with macaroni salad. Enjoy."

Harper watched as we took our first bites, then reveled in our groans of satisfaction. Jean-Pierre called us *beasts* for making such noises and retreated to the kitchen.

Harper waited a few more bites before asking, "Did you guys stop by just for food? You know you're always welcome here, but I have to get another recipe intro done before the supper rush, so I can't talk long."

I choked on my food at the mention of yet another recipe intro that I would need to read. When I recovered, I said, "We do have a few questions for you." I wiped my hands before pulling my notebook from my pocket. "Have you ever heard of a Nexellum cast iron skillet?"

"Yes, I've heard of it, but I don't use that brand."

"Why not?"

"It's a cheaper brand that needs more maintenance," Harper explained. "It's fine for home chefs that can season it between uses. It doesn't work well at a restaurant where it has to be cleaned and reused multiple times a night."

"Is it an exclusive brand? Something we can use to track down an owner?"

"No," she said. "Anyone can get them at Walmart, garage sales, or thrift stores."

Sophia and I exchanged glances. Cathy said the same thing to us from her perch in the green dumpster.

"What about a ProEdge butcher knife?" I continued. "Is that a traceable brand?"

"Again, no. It may be called *Pro*Edge but a cheap knife like that wouldn't make it a day in a professional kitchen."

I wiped my mouth again then threw the napkin on my empty plate. "Damn, I thought that may be a lead."

"Sorry I couldn't be more helpful," Harper said. "Is cookware the only connection you have between the two murders?"

"Dawson is the only one that thinks these murders are connected," Sophia said. "I don't agree, though."

"Well, Sophia thinks our murderer is a girl," I retorted pettily. "She said you could be our murderer, Harper."

"Me?" Harper turned to Sophia. "What did I ever do to you to make you think I'm a murderer?"

"That's not what I said! I said our suspect is a thin person that could be a woman. I was just using you as an example. He conveniently left out that I put you in a group with Hilary Swank and Cate Blanchett."

"Ooh, I love Hilary Swank," Harper said, once again Sophia's best friend. "She was so amazing in *Million Dollar Baby*."

"*Anyway*," I interrupted, "We thought that if the weapons were high end enough that they could be traced to whoever purchased them, it would help us decide if I'm right."

Harper shot Sophia the *look* before turning to me. "Cast iron skillets are used in most American-type cooking, especially in the South. Pretty much every kitchen in America has one, so that wouldn't be very helpful. What does the knife look like? A 'butcher knife' can actually mean half a dozen different styles and uses of knives."

"It was the big rectangular one," Sophia said. "Not a pointy one."

Harper furrowed her eyebrows. "Those are technically meat cleavers. That's a weird choice."

"What makes you say that?" I leaned forward eagerly.

"Well, most people use sharp, pointy knives because they do the most damage, right?" She waited for us to nod in agreement. "A cleaver would take more work and power to do the same."

"It would still be deadly, though," Sophia said.

"Of course, it would. A cleaver can go through bone, which is obviously painful," Harper explained. "But it won't hit the vital organs right away. So, unless it was used on the neck to make your victim bleed out, or deep into the brain, it would've been a slow, painful death."

Sophia turned to me. "That backs up what Cathy said about the cause of death."

"Thanks for the help, love," I said, pulling her into a hug. In her ear I whispered, "I'm so turned on by you right now."

She laughed and pushed me away. "I'm glad I could help, but I need to get back to work. The intro won't write itself."

Sophia stacked the dishes while I wiped the counter with a wet rag. We'd said our goodbyes and turned toward the door when Harper called out for me. "Dawson, do you mind helping me move a filing cabinet in my office before you leave. I'd ask Jean-Pierre, but I wouldn't want to mess up his manicure."

I gave Sophia the car keys so she could get the air conditioner going, then I followed Harper to her office. As we passed through the kitchen, her staff was busy preparing for the dinner rush. In her office, I crossed to the file cabinet and tested the weight.

"Where are we moving this to?" I asked.

"Over here, please."

I turned to see where she was indicating. Instead, I saw her sitting on her desk, her blouse unbuttoned, and her skirt pulled up to her thighs. She winked at me and licked her lips. I crossed to her and hungrily took her on the edge of her desk. As we climaxed, she smothered my cry with her hand and stifled hers by biting my shoulder. We held each other after, her legs still around me, both of us breathing hard.

"I thought the honeymoon phase was supposed to wear off?" I asked as I pulled up my pants.

"A three-year honeymoon isn't so bad, is it?"

"I'm not complaining," I laughed. "You have to get back to work, though.

Will you be home late tonight?"

"It shouldn't be too late," she said, buttoning her blouse. "We've got full staff tonight, so cleanup should be easy."

"Good, it'll be nice for us to have a quiet night in."

I gave her another long, deep kiss before leaving the office. Jean-Pierre was leaning against a wall, doing a poor job pretending he didn't know what we were doing. He gave me a cheeky smile.

"*That's* why she keeps me around," I said to him.

* * * *

I didn't leave the station until after 9:00. I wasn't sure if Harper would be home from the restaurant before me, but her little green truck was already parked in the garage when I pulled in. I practically ran into the house, hoping for another desk-top tryst. I tossed my keys and briefcase onto the kitchen island. The keys skidded across the slick surface and clinked against a porcelain bowl.

The clinking was loud in the eerie quiet of the house. Usually, our home had a constant cadence of noise. I always had the TV going with a documentary or sports. Harper liked to listen to all genres of music at full volume. And, of course, when she cooked, Harper talked to herself over the cacophony of banging, chopping, and sizzling. Tonight, though, there was pure silence.

I turned to the porcelain bowl and saw the pack of Ramen noodles inside. I never pressured Harper to have meals prepared for me, though I had come to expect them. I knew this display meant I was in trouble for something. A look at what lay under the bowl told me why.

A dozen manuscripts. A thick pile of paper with the intros to Harper's recipes. The ones that I had promised to read, that I had been lying about having read, that I had stashed in my bedside table until I could find the time. I had been busted and I had no one to blame but myself.

I picked up the pile and headed to Harper's office. I peeked through the small gap in the doorway to see her sitting at her desk. Her glasses were on, and her hair was messy as though she had been running her hands through it in frustration. She was working through a stack of papers, scribbling furiously with a red pen. If I weren't in so much trouble, I would've been turned on by the sexy librarian look.

I knocked gently on the door. She glanced up for a split second before returning to her papers. She was ignoring me, but she didn't tell me to go away. I took that as an invitation to enter. I sat in the leather chair across from her and waited for her to speak.

"Did you enjoy your supper?" she asked, not pausing her work.

"I decided to increase my punishment and starve instead," I quipped.

"If all you're going to do is make jokes, then just leave," she snarled. "I've got too much work to do to be distracted by you."

"I'm sorry, Harper, I know I promised to read these, but—"

"But you got busy at work?" she lashed out. "You had other things come up? You have a career? I couldn't possibly understand any of that."

"You know I don't think that," I said, raising my voice slightly. "You know I support your work and help you out as much as I can."

"As much as you can, huh? You've read, what, three of them? Four? If that's as *much* as you can do, you might as well not help at all," she said. Pointing at the stack in my hand, she spat, "They aren't even very long!"

"I know they're not. You just kept giving them to me at bad times. I really did mean to get back to them."

"But you're too busy." She threw the pen down on the desk. "Yet, when you show up at my restaurant, I take the time to make you and your partner lunch *and* help you with your case. Hell, I even took a few minutes to screw you in my office!"

"You enjoyed that as much as I did!" I shot back.

"Keep dreaming," she snapped.

I bit my tongue. I didn't want to say something I would regret, especially when I knew I was in the wrong. "I know I messed up, and I'm sorry," I begged. "You know I've always supported you. I'm going to read these. Tonight."

"Don't bother," she growled.

She picked up her pen and started working again. I left her office with my tail between my legs. I would stay up all night if it meant I finished this stack. I retreated to the living room and sat in the most uncomfortable chair in the house. It was the only way to keep my eyes open.

I made it through the first four quickly. Poland, France, Australia, and Greece. They sounded like such beautiful places. I was familiar with several of the foods she mentioned in the intros. It was making me hungry to see the menu she was creating. I briefly contemplated cooking the packet of Ramen noodles but thought better of it. My stomach could wait until I had finished every story.

I did everything I could for the next four hours to stay awake. I paced the house, I snapped a rubber band on my wrist, I even smacked my face. I had to reread many paragraphs because my eyes weren't transferring the words to my brain. I struggled to keep my eyes open even though the stories were cute and quirky and showed who Harper was as a chef and a person.

I was leaning against the kitchen island, my face in my hands and my elbows on the granite. I dozed off for just a second. My elbow slipped off the edge and my face smacked the countertop. I was suddenly wide awake. I glanced at the clock on the stove and realized it was 2:30 am. I had been asleep for longer than a second. I rubbed my face, then moved back to the uncomfortable chair in which I had started. I only had three left. I could do this!

Hands ran across my shoulders and down my arm. Harper grabbed the last of the intros and set it on the end table beside me. "That's enough for tonight," she whispered. "Let's get some sleep."

She pulled me from the chair and led me to the bedroom. Cocooned in the cool silk sheets, she whispered, "You know I'll always love you, right?"

"Do you promise?"

"Cross my heart and hope to die," she said, sealing it with a kiss.

What's in a Name?

During my four months in France, I focused on my skills as a *patissier*. That is, a pastry chef. *Patissiers* have extensive training in desserts and sweets. In Europe, it is common for fine dining establishments to hire pastry chefs specifically to handle desserts, palate cleansers, and specialty sweets.

As excited as I was to get started—and to spend months indulging my sweet tooth for the sake of education—I got off on the wrong foot with my training chef. I worked in the heart of Paris at a *patisserie* called *Nourrir Mon Ame*, or, Nourish My Soul. I was greeted by a young shop worker named Giselle, who introduced me to the chef's assistant, Etienne. After a quick kitchen tour, Etienne introduced me to the boss, Kevin.

I burst out laughing, thinking the name was a joke. I was surrounded by the most stereotypical French names. I wasn't expecting a regular, American-sounding name for the *pâtissier* in France's most famous bakery. Kevin didn't see the humor.

I apologized profusely, but he didn't accept. He ordered me to make enough puff pastry to fill the shelves and custom orders of over 40 dozen croissants. And it had to be done that night before I was allowed to leave. It was an archaic culinary punishment of folding, rolling, and rotating.

It took several weeks for Kevin to warm up to me. And it wasn't because I was exceptionally gifted at pastries or desserts. It was because I was willing to admit my shortcomings, ask for help, and be teachable.

Our bond solidified the night I almost set myself on fire. I was trying to crisp the top of my crème brûlée, a recipe I had been working on for weeks to perfect. For the first time since I'd arrived, Kevin complimented my dessert unprompted. I was so startled that I straightened up to look at him—and set my hair on fire with the torch!

He grabbed the nearest container of liquid: a cup of creamer! He splashed it on me without hesitation. I was stunned at first, but as the cream dripped down my chef's coat, I burst out laughing. So did Kevin.

We got along well for the rest of my training, and our mutual respect grew. I still make Kevin's crème brûlée recipe at least once a month at my restaurant.

Crème Brûlée

PREP TIME: 10 mins   COOK TIME: 30 mins
TOTAL TIME: 40 mins   SERVINGS: 4 servings

INGREDIENTS
- 2 cups heavy creme
- 4 egg yolks
- ⅓ cup sugar
- 1 teaspoon vanilla
- ¼ cup sugar for topping

INSTRUCTIONS
- In large measuring cup (or easy-to-pour bowl) whisk egg yolks, ⅓ cup sugar, and vanilla together.
- In small pan, heat cream over medium heat until bubbles appear along the edge of the pan. (DO NOT BOIL)
- When cream is hot, slowly add it to egg yolk mixture, whisking continually.
- Pour into 4 wide and shallow ramekins.
- Place ramekins in baking dish. Fill baking dish with hot water until it comes ¾ of the way up the side of the ramekins. Be careful not to get water inside the ramekins.
- Bake at 325° for 30-45 minutes. Adjust times for ramekins as needed (deeper dish = longer bake). Custard should be set on top, but still jiggle under crust.
- Cool to room temperature, then put in refrigerator for 2 hours.
- When completely cooled, sprinkle each custard with 1 tablespoon sugar and use torch or oven broiler until top is caramelized and brown.

Chapter 10
Ling Chan

D ammit," I swore under my breath. "No rain all damn summer, but the *one time* I walk somewhere, there's a downpour."

I was standing inside the pharmacy, looking out the big windows into the downpour. I wasn't dressed for rain! I wasn't wearing a coat because it's August in Nebraska, where it's 100° during the day and 90° at night. I didn't have an umbrella because it's August in Nebraska, where the only thing wet coming from the sky is bird poop! And I didn't drive here because the doctor told me I needed to increase my exercise and pick up my prescription, so this killed two birds with one stone. It didn't have anything to do with it being August in Nebraska, but it serves me right for trying to follow the doctor's orders!

"Ling, are you going to be all right out there in the storm?" Joanie, the pharmacist, yelled from the counter at the back of the store.

"I'm going to be wet and grumpy, but I'll be fine," I called. To myself I said, "I think."

"Do you want me to give you a ride?" she called again. "We close in 20 minutes. I could give you a ride home."

"No, Joanie, I don't want to be any trouble," I replied.

"If you change your mind, you come back, ok," she said. "I don't want you to get hurt trying to get home."

"I'll be careful, Joanie," I tried to reassure her. "I'm just going to wait a few more minutes to see if there's a lull."

"All right, young man," she said. "You be careful out there."

It was going to take me at least half an hour to get back to my apartment.

I'd had surgery on my back more than six months ago, so running wasn't an option. I was still in so much pain, that the best I could hope for was a quick shuffle. I was going to be glad to have the refill of OxyContin when I got home.

When the next rumble of thunder rattled the windows, I decided to go before the storm got even worse. I pushed open the door, the happy jingling of the bells above the door was a stark contrast to the angry storm raging just outside. Before I made it to the end of the block, I was sopping wet. My jeans kept slipping down my hips because of the extra water weight. I shoved my prescription into my pocket so I could hold my pants up with both hands. My sandals became wet and slippery, causing me to stumble repeatedly. Each lurch sent pain shooting up my spine and down both legs. Within another block, I was exhausted from the effort. I reached the next storefront awning and leaned against the building to rest.

I closed my eyes and took deep breaths, willing the pain to dissipate. I couldn't take another pain pill for a few hours, but I was tempted to disobey my doctor's orders and take one now. After all, following doctor's orders is why I was stuck in the rain in the first place! I forgot about the pain when I heard the most beautiful laugh float toward me through the rain.

In a flash of lightning, I saw a woman standing on the sidewalk, away from the protection of an awning. Her arms were outstretched, and her head thrown back as she twirled slowly. The glow of a streetlamp caught the droplets as they bounced off her, creating an ethereal glow around her. When I finally saw her face, I saw pure joy. She looked like the happiest woman in the world, standing out there in the pouring rain.

I couldn't take my eyes off her. She was tall and thin and wore a black sundress with a wide belt on her waist. The dress was soaked and stuck to her body. Her arms and legs were toned, her skin pale. She was wearing a floppy sun hat that hung limp and wet around her face. And what a beautiful face it was! She had a fine jawline and prominent cheekbones. But it was her big, bright eyes that really captivated me.

When those eyes met mine, I felt like I'd been hit by lightning. She stared straight at me like she knew who I was. Like she had been waiting for me. She smiled that beautiful smile and walked toward me. I was tempted to get up and shuffle away, but my back still hurt too much. More than that, I *wanted* to stay, and wanted her to come talk to me. I wanted to know her.

She approached me, looking me up and down, sizing me up. I was worried she wouldn't like what she saw. I'm second-generation Chinese-American, and

I was used to being rejected by women. Most women like tall men, and I'm only 5' 6"; they like muscular men, and I'm scrawny; they like facial hair, and the only extra hair on my face is between my eyebrows; they like big, expressive eyes, and mine are small and dark. I didn't hold it against them that I wasn't their type, but I had just gotten used to it.

"Do you mind if I sit?" she asked.

"No, no, of course not," I answered.

"I love rainstorms. Don't you?"

I stared at her dumbly, then blurted, "I'm all wet."

She giggled. "I noticed. But the rain is so refreshing. It makes plants green and cleans off buildings." She took a deep breath through her nose. "And the air smells so fresh."

"You sound like a fortune cookie," I said. Then I slapped my head, realizing what a stupid thing that was to say.

"I'm okay with that." She looked thoughtful for a minute, then stated, "Now I want Chinese food."

"Is that because I'm Chinese?"

"That is merely a coincidence," she reassured me. "It's mentioning the fortune cookie that sparked the craving."

"There's a good takeout place around the corner," I volunteered. "They've got the best pork dumplings and fried rice in Omaha."

"Sounds delicious." She stood up abruptly and started walking. Before she left the cover of the awning, she turned and looked at me curiously. "Aren't you coming?"

I pointed at myself, like an idiot, and said, "You mean me?"

"Yes, you."

"You want me to come with you?"

"You did suggest it, after all." She stuck her hand back out into the rain. "Besides, I don't want to enjoy the rain alone."

I jumped up, instantly regretting it as pain shot up my spine. I tried to act like nothing was wrong, though. "My name's Ling Chan, by the way."

"It's wonderful to meet you, Ling Chan. I'm Cass."

We didn't talk on our way to Miss Yang's Oriental Cuisine. It wasn't an uncomfortable silence, though. We just listened to the rain and the thunder. If this had been a date, it would have been the best date I'd ever had. But I knew I'd probably never see Cass again. I had to enjoy it while it lasted.

At the restaurant, I greeted Miss Yang in Cantonese. She asked about my 'girlfriend,' but I told her she was just a friend. I had been coming to Miss Yang's at least once a week for the three years I'd lived in the Old Market, but I was always alone. Miss Yang had played matchmaker for her children and tried to do the same for me over the years. I know she meant well, but I wasn't interested in being set up.

I ordered my usual beef and broccoli, while Cass ordered cashew chicken with an order of fried rice. Then she added pork dumplings. I was surprised when she pulled out her wallet and handed Miss Yang cash to cover the meal, including a generous tip.

"You don't have to pay for me," I said.

"Nonsense. I invited you." Then she turned to Miss Yang. "The name for the ticket is Cass. *Xièxiè.*"

While we waited for our food, Cass picked up a menu printed with the Chinese Zodiac and asked me what year I was born. I told her 1997.

"The year of the Ox. People born this year are gentle, hardworking, reliable, and patient." She eyed me closely. "Does that accurately describe you, Ling?"

"It's pretty close, I think. But that chart is missing that most Ox are also materialistic and stubborn, so watch out," I teased.

She continued reading through all the different animals. A flash of curly hair in the kitchen's pass-through window caught my attention. Miss Yang was peeking at us and giggling whenever Cass touched my arm or shoulder. I knew she was hoping that I had finally found a match. I admitted to myself that I hoped she was right.

Ten minutes later—much longer than it usually took to prepare an order— Miss Yang reappeared with our to-go containers. She told me in Cantonese to make sure I didn't let Cass get away.

"*Fàngxīn, wǒ bù huì ràng tā pǎo diào de,*" Cass said in decent Cantonese. *Don't worry, I won't let him get away.*

Miss Yang giggled before bustling off to the kitchen, yelling over her shoulder that Cass is a keeper. I followed Cass back out into the rain. We hustled to a bus stop, where we could enjoy the rain under the protection of the glass shelter and straddled the bench to use it as a table.

"I was not expecting you to know Cantonese," I said as I unpacked the food.

"I spent a semester abroad in Hong Kong," she explained. "I'm not fluent, but I knew enough to get by back then. I'm just as surprised as you are that I remembered any."

"My grandparents live in Hong Kong. We used to visit them for a long vacation every few years. My father only allows us to speak Cantonese in his house."

She picked up a full bite of fried rice with her chopsticks and popped it in her mouth. "You were right; this is amazing," she said through a mouthful. "Tell me more about you, Ling."

"There's not much to tell," I said. "I'm 25 and work in computer programming."

"How very Asian of you," she teased.

"It was that or medicine, and I don't like blood. People would've died."

"I think you made the right choice, then." She reached over and snagged a broccoli floret. "No significant others? No pets? No kids?"

"Nope, none of those. I work too many hours to have time for any of that."

She raised an eyebrow. "Yet you have time for impromptu dates with a stranger?"

I choked on my beef at the mention of a *date*. "This wasn't planned. I just needed to pick up a prescription for pain meds. I meant to pick them up two days ago, so this meeting is purely chance." Though she didn't ask, I felt the need to clarify, "I got hurt and had to have surgery a few months ago. I'm not, like, addicted to painkillers or anything, though. I take them as prescribed."

"You don't seem like the drug addict type, anyway," she said, matter-of-factly. "Besides your zodiac would be wrong if you were. Most addicts aren't hard working or reliable."

"Well, um, thank you."

"What kind of accident were you in? If you don't mind my asking."

"No, it's fine. It wasn't anything spectacular, though. It's actually kind of embarrassing."

"I won't laugh. Cross my heart and hope to die." She made an X with her chopsticks and held it over her heart.

I suddenly felt comfortable with her. I felt I could tell her anything pitiful or painful, and she would accept it. She wouldn't judge or try to fix it or tell me what I should do. She would just listen and understand.

"I hurt myself trying to deadlift at the gym," I said sheepishly. "I liked a girl at work and overheard her talking about how much she liked muscled guys, so I did a trial membership at a gym. Of course, I had no idea what I was doing. I just tried to copy another guy. I had too much weight on the bar and when I tried to lift it, I herniated three discs in my lower back."

"That sounds painful," she said, finishing her cashew chicken.

"It was the most painful thing I'd ever felt," I agreed. "I had to have corrective surgery a few weeks later. It's been almost six months now and I'm still not back to normal. Most days are fine, but other days I just want to lie in bed and sleep to avoid the pain."

"Is that why you were leaning against that building like James Dean? Because your back hurts?"

I laughed at the idea as I gathered our empty containers into the plastic bag. "I'm no James Dean. I'm not that good-looking."

"Don't sell yourself short."

She was looking at me with such an earnest expression. She leaned toward me, and I could tell she wanted to kiss me. I wanted to kiss her, too, so I copied her. Our lips were almost touching when pain surged through my back!

I cried out and fell forward, barely catching myself before face-planting between her legs. I breathed deeply and tried to push myself upright. I felt her hands gently push on my shoulders, helping me up. I struggled to pull the OxyContin bottle from my pocket. When I finally did, my hands were shaking too much to open it. Cass reached over and took the bottle, popping the lid off.

"How many?" she asked.

"Just-just one," I stammered.

She tipped it into my hand, then held the straw from my drink to my mouth. I swallowed the pill, willing it to work quickly.

"Thank you," I whispered.

"Oxy's," Cass said. "That's pretty potent stuff. Are you sure you're not an addict?"

I tried to laugh at her joke, but I was in too much pain.

"What can I do to help now?"

"I should try to get back to my apartment to lie down. It's only about six blocks." I tried to stand up, but the pain made my legs buckle.

"Ok, we're not going anywhere," she said definitively. "Come on, lay back."

She helped me turn around and ease back onto the bench. She put my head in her lap and stroked my hair while she talked about stars and galaxies. I wasn't listening, just enjoying the feel of her hands combing slowly through my hair, the warmth of her body against me, and the sound of the rainfall harmonizing with her voice.

I drifted off to sleep in her lap. When I awoke, the rain had slowed to a drizzle. There was still moisture in the air, creating an aura of light around the streetlamps. When Cass leaned over me, there was a light halo around her face.

"You're so beautiful," I blurted out.

"And you're so handsome."

I tried sitting up and was relieved that the pain in my back had reduced to a dull throb. I still wanted to go home but I wanted her to go with me.

"Would you... Would you like to come back to my place?"

"That's very forward of you," she said. But she didn't seem upset.

"I-I didn't mean... I just want to keep talking to you. Nothing else."

She thought for a minute. "How about we let the fortune cookie decide?"

Cass dug the fortune cookies from the bag and cracked one open. She read it, but her face didn't give anything away.

"So, what's my fortune?" I asked nervously.

Her face was serious when she read, "*If you want the rainbow, you have to learn to dance in the rain.*"

"You've already played in the rain," I reminded her. "I think that would count as dancing."

"I think you're right," she agreed. "Let's go find us a rainbow."

Cass helped me to my feet. She slung my arm around her shoulders and put her arm around my waist. She pulled me close as we walked slowly toward my apartment. As I leaned on her, she supported me without question.

When we got closer to my block, I suddenly realized that the entrance to my apartment could be featured in a serial killer documentary. It starts with a walk down a poorly lit alley to the back of a converted warehouse. My car happened to be parked there, waiting for me to throw her into the trunk and drive away. If she went that far, we would then climb the exterior stairs to get to my second-floor apartment. Even worse, the stairs were crudely enclosed with plywood. Inside the death trap, there was only one exposed bulb at the top of the stairs. Dim alley to dark stairwell to dingy apartment. It screamed *this is where I kill you.*

When I turned us into the alley, I saw her eyes begin to dart around. No doubt she was planning her escape route or looking for places someone could be hiding. But she didn't stop moving. She didn't even stop talking. It wasn't until we got to the rear of the building, and I'd dug my keys out of my pocket that she stood away from me.

"You don't have to come up if you don't want to," I whispered.

"I do! Want to, I mean," she said nervously. "I just don't know if I should."

It was my turn to hesitate. I didn't want to push her, but I really wanted her to come with me. "How about we let the other fortune cookie decide?" I suggested.

"Great idea." She cracked it open and smiled. *"Don't be afraid to take chances when the opportunity of a lifetime appears."*

I smiled at my good fortune. She stepped closer to me. This was it; she was finally going to kiss me. Her eyes sparkled as they had when she twirled in the rain. Then her face changed. The sparkle was gone, a menacing scowl replacing it. I felt a sharp pain in one ear, then another in my eye.

Train through Poland

My trip to Poland was one of my least favorite. Not because I didn't meet great people or learn a lot, but because I barely got to see the country. Most of what I did see swept by a window at 100 mph as I worked in the catering car of a luxury passenger train. The train tour stopped at many of the major cities in Poland, such as Krakow, Warsaw, and Gdansk. We served over 100 passengers and crew for the ten-day tour.

This situation presented a unique culinary opportunity. We had to create three meals per day, with at least two options per meal and substitutions for dietary restrictions. We couldn't repeat the menu for ten days, either. And we did it all with a skeleton crew in a train car with less than 2000 square feet for the kitchen, freezer, and dry-good storage.

It taught me more about running a kitchen than any other stop on my journey. The head chef had to figure out how to make so many different dishes using primarily the same ingredients. There wasn't enough storage room to have a meat or vegetable that was in only one recipe. I also learned how to find each person's strengths and weaknesses. With such a small crew, we had to ensure every task was done quickly and up to standard. No time for training while prepping for a meal.

My favorite person the entire trip, and one of my true best friends, was a young Polish girl named Lena. She was taking her gap year before starting university and decided to visit her country more in-depth as a waitress in the premier dining car. She was exceptionally smart, spoke five languages, and could tell you anything you wanted to know about Greek mythology. She aspired to be a doctor despite her family's disapproval. They wanted her to go to business school and then go back home to work at the family's bagel shop.

A little research told me that her parent's "little bagel shop" was actually the best-selling bagel shop in all of Warsaw. I wanted so badly to ask her to teach me to make those bagels. But I also wanted to respect her desire to be her own person. Luckily, we came to care for each other so much that she taught me to make *Bajgle Feniksa*, Phoenix Bagels.

Polish Bagel

PREP TIME: 2 hrs 10 mins
TOTAL TIME: 3 hrs

COOK TIME: 25 mins
SERVINGS: 4 servings

INGREDIENTS
- 1¼ cups warm water
- 2 tablespoons white sugar
- 2 tablespoons active dry yeast
- 3½ - 4 cups bread flour
- 1½ teaspoon salt
- 1 egg white whisked with 1 tablespoon water

INSTRUCTIONS
- Combine warm water, sugar and yeast into a stand mixer or large bowl. Let sit until all is dissolved, about 5 minutes.
- Add flour and salt. Mix thoroughly by hand or with dough hook on mixer until stiff dough forms.
- Cover dough in oil and place in large bowl. Cover loosely with clean cloth and let dough rise in warm, draft-free place until doubled in size.
- When dough has doubled, punch it down and place on lightly floured surface.
- Divide dough into 8 pieces, weighing to ensure even size. Roll dough into ball and flatten gently.
- Press hole into middle of ball, then stretch into an even ring.
- Place shaped dough on cookie sheet and cover with damp cloth to rest for 10 minutes.
- Pour water into saucepan and bring to boil. Cook each dough ring for 45 seconds on each side. (Longer boil = chewier)
- Remove bagel with spoon and place on paper towel to drain.
- Brush each bagel with egg mixture and add desired toppings.
- Bake at 425° for 20-25 minutes until golden brown.

Chapter 11

On Wednesday, Sophia and I sat at our desks, trying to be busy. We hadn't had any new breaks in the case, so we were reviewing all the evidence, hoping to find something new. Sophia was still clicking through pictures from the Scottish-Irish Festival, but I had given up on the footage from Barn Sour. I had looked through all of it, from the whole month, several times. There was no chance that I had missed something.

Instead of driving myself crazy, I decided to reset my brain by focusing on something else for a while. I reached into my briefcase and pulled out one of Harper's intros. I kept all of them with me at all times just for moments like this. She was still giving them to me at a steady pace, and this was the only way I would be able to keep up.

I was almost done with a story about the family Harper had lived and worked with in Scotland after she graduated from culinary school when Sophia's cell phone rang.

"Leoni," Sophia answered. "Since when do you give out the assignments, Cathy?"

I perked up. We usually got our cases from Chief Probst. It must be something amusing—or terrible—for Cathy to be making the call.

"Chopsticks? But how?" Sophia turned and looked at me, her eyes huge with excitement. "The eye and the ear?"

"Another body?" I whispered to her.

Sophia nodded. "We'll be right there."

"What do we have?" I asked, grabbing my cell phone and car keys from the desk.

"You'll see," she said coyly. "You're going to hate this one!"

Twenty minutes later, I saw why. Rather, I smelled why. The victim's deco

Decomposing body had been shoved between a parked car and the wall of a building. He had been there for a week or more based on the smell alone. The body's bloating and dark red color also indicated it had been exposed to the 100° heat and elements for some time. That was saying nothing of the condition of the exposed skin, which rats and other wildlife had nibbled on.

The most concerning part of the body was the two 10" wooden chop- sticks protruding from his head. One was jammed into his ear. The other was in his eye at an upward angle, deep enough into his brain that only an inch of the stick was still visible.

"It's making my head hurt just looking at it," Sophia said.

"I bet it didn't tickle," I agreed. "With one in his brain, I hope he didn't suffer very long."

"Incorrect, Detective," Cathy said from behind me. "Even though it's in the brain, chances are it still took the vic a few minutes to die. And the one in his ear? Mr. Chan felt every second of that excruciating pain."

"Mr. Chan?" I asked. "Did you find an ID?"

"We already bagged the wallet," Cathy replied. "It had his ID, credit cards, and cash. It didn't look like anything was taken."

I glanced at the deformed body. "Are we sure this is our guy?"

"We will need dental records to confirm, but based on height, hair, and eye color, we're pretty certain it's him. The listed address on his license is this building, too. It looks like someone jumped him when he got home."

Sophia hadn't stopped looking at the chopsticks. "If I were in that much pain," she shuddered at the thought, "I would've screamed."

"Me, too. What are you thinking?" I asked.

Sophia pointed to the end of the ally. "That's one of the main roads in the Old Market. The stores are open until 9:00 pm, and during the summer there are people walking around until late at night. How did nobody hear him scream?"

"Maybe he was smothered?" I offered. "Hand over the mouth or some sort of gag?"

"It's possible," Cathy agreed. "I won't know until I do his autopsy. But I should have the results back for you by tomorrow."

"Do we have an approximate date of death?" I asked.

Cathy shook her head. "It's hard to tell. A few days, maybe a week? The heat accelerates decomposition, so an exact date is impossible. You'll have to figure that out on your end."

Sophia and I stepped out of the alley to get away from the stench.

"Chopsticks!" Sophia exclaimed. "I didn't even know chopsticks could be used as a murder weapon!"

"It's a new one for sure," I said. "But it's another kitchen utensil."

"Is it, though?" she asked skeptically. "Is it really?"

"It's not a frying pan or a knife, but I think it still counts as a kitchen utensil."

"I don't know, Dawson. You were stretching a little on the last one, but you're stretching a lot on this one."

I gave her a pointed look. Before I could argue, Cathy called us from the alley.

"Detectives, I think I've got something here!" she yelled.

We hurried back down the alley. Cathy's team had just lifted the body into a bag and onto a gurney. Cathy was staring at the ground where the body had been, a big smile on her face. I followed her gaze but saw nothing besides bugs and flattened grass.

"Look," Cathy whispered conspiratorially.

"What are we looking at, Cathy?" I asked.

"It's wet," she pointed out.

"Gross," Sophia said. "Body fluids?"

"Not likely," Cathy said. "The ground was wet when he was put there. It must have rained shortly before he was killed."

"When was the last time it rained?" Sophia asked.

"Last Wednesday," I said.

Sophia looked shocked. "You answered that fast. How do you know that?"

"Because I, umm, know everything?" I couldn't tell them about coming home to Harper naked by the washing machine.

"There's obviously a story there," Cathy said. "Anyway, that time frame lines up with the state of decomposition."

"That would also explain why no one heard anything; no one would've been on the streets if it was raining."

I pointed to the clear evidence bag Cathy was holding. "What's that?"

"We found these in his pocket," she said. "He was taking the good stuff."

Inside the bag was a pill bottle labeled **OxyContin 30 mg, 180 count. Take 1 pill every 4 hours as needed for pain.** The prescription was for **Chan, Ling**.

"Mr. Chan must have been in serious pain even before getting chopsticked,"

Sophia said.

"We have a wallet with cash and credit cards and a nearly full bottle of drugs. This wasn't a robbery." I turned to Sophia. "That's been the case at all three crime scenes. All the victims had money and other valuables and could easily have been robberies gone bad."

"I agree; I don't think robbery was the motive," Sophia said. "Grace had a credit card and cash in her wallet that wasn't touched. If this prescription is full, the street value of Oxy is over $1500."

"Callum had almost ten grand on him, but it was hidden," I reminded her. "It wouldn't have taken very long to find it if our guy wanted to. If robbery isn't the motive, what is?"

Sophia grabbed the bagged pill bottle from Cathy and inspected it. "It looks like the pharmacy is only a few blocks away," Sophia said. "Let's go talk to them."

The pharmacy was a small mom-and-pop store with trinkets, cards, and over-the-counter medications. We found an employee and asked for the owner, and were directed to Joanie, the pharmacist. We showed her our badges and dropped the evidence bag on the counter.

"What can you tell us about this?" I asked.

She picked up the bag, turning it so the little pills fell as it rotated. She read the name and typed it into her computer. "Ling filled and picked up the prescription seven days ago. I'm the one that helped him. It looks like he took one, maybe two."

"You can tell by looking at it?" I asked skeptically.

"I'm a pharmacist, Detective. It's my job," she sneered. "Besides, I've known Ling for years. He had back surgery six months ago after an accident. He takes his medications exactly as prescribed and picks up his refill every 30 days. He never asks for it sooner."

"Do you remember if it was raining the night he picked this up?" Sophia asked.

"Yes, it was downpouring. I felt bad for Ling. He wasn't dressed for the rain." A look of realization crossed her face. "Something happened to Ling, didn't it?"

Sophia nodded. "Unfortunately, his body was found this morning outside of his apartment."

"That's horrible!" Joanie exclaimed. "He was such a sweet young man. I tried to set him up with my daughter several times, but he wasn't interested.

He was too shy."

"Have you ever seen him with anyone?" I asked. "Man, woman, relative?"

"No, he's always alone." She started crying. "I offered him a ride home that night, but he said he'd be fine."

"Do you offer your customers rides often?" I asked.

"No, never. But Ling can't move very well because of his back. I was worried he would slip and fall and hurt himself."

We thanked her for her time and then left the pharmacy. We canvassed all the local businesses as we returned to the crime scene. We got the same story at the dry cleaners, a video game store, and a convenience store: Ling was a chronically single loner and never went out with friends or family. Our luck changed at the Chinese restaurant, Miss Yang's Oriental Cuisine.

"Ling ordered beef and broccoli like always," she told us in slightly broken English. "And fried rice. He says I have best fried rice in Omaha."

"Has he ever been here with anyone else?" I asked.

"Not until last week. He showed up with beautiful woman," she said.

"A woman?"

"Yes, and she is smart, too. Spoke to me in Cantonese. I like her." She smiled approvingly.

"Any chance you have security cameras inside?"

"No, no cameras," she shook her head. "Too expensive. This good neighborhood; don't need them."

"Was there anything specific you can tell us about this young woman?"

She thought for a moment. "Not good hips for having babies. Otherwise, standard Nebraska girl. Her name is Cass."

Sophia and I stiffened. *Cass* was the same name reported by witnesses at both Grace and Callum's murders.

"You're certain this was a woman? Any chance it was just a feminine man?" I pushed.

"Yes, it was a woman. She wore black dress and hat. Her skinny legs had no hair. She had boy haircut, though, very short."

"How do you know her name was Cass?" I asked. "Do you have a credit card receipt with her name on it?"

"No, sorry, but—" she began rummaging through paperwork under the counter. When she stood up, she held a ticket printed with an order and the name CASS written in all capital letters. "Take this."

I looked at the receipt. The name could be a fake given by the suspect, but it was one hell of a coincidence. The bottom of the ticket showed the date and time of the transaction: Wednesday, 7:41 pm. I took the ticket as evidence, and we left the restaurant.

"I *told* you it was a woman!" Sophia bragged when we were back out on the sidewalk. "I was right!"

"I want to believe you," I said, "But like you told me, show me the evidence."

"I'm telling you, Dawson, a woman is doing this." The smile left her face as another thought dawned on her. "That means we are looking in the wrong suspect pool!"

* * * *

Thursday, Sophia was already sitting at her desk when I got to work. Judging by the mess of candy and energy bar wrappers, she had been there all night, fueling herself with a pure sugar high. She didn't greet me when I sat at my desk.

"Sophia, good morning," I said.

She didn't respond. She stared at her laptop, eyes wide, pupils dilated, mumbling under her breath. I waved a hand in front of her face, and she jumped. She pulled her earbuds from her ears and swore at me.

"Holy shit, Dawson, you scared me!" she yelled. "What the hell do you think you're doing?"

"I could ask you the same thing," I replied. "How long have you been here?"

"Depends what time it is."

I glanced at my phone. "It's 8:05."

"Then I've been here—" she calculated on her fingers, "Fifteen hours. Give or take."

"Fifteen hours! Sophia, that's all night *after* we worked a full shift yesterday."

"And?"

"And you need to go home and get some rest," I said.

"I'm fine, I promise. I've just been going through the databases looking for our suspect."

"Which databases are you using?"

"All of them," she said, her eyes glued on the screen again.

"What do you mean, all of them?"

114

She growled at me. "I mean, I'm using all of them: Nebraska, Ohio, South Dakota, Kansas, and Missouri. I even called a friend from Chicago and got her to look into things in Illinois, just in case. And then there are the federal databases; VICAP, CODIS, Interpol, and—"

She was frenzied now, talking too fast and waving her hands. Her face was turning a concerning shade of red and her eyes were so wide her irises were ringed with white. I worried she would have a stroke if she didn't calm down.

"Sophia. Sophia!" I grabbed her by the shoulders and made her look at me. "I need you to take a few deep breaths."

She did—three giant, gulping breaths. I watched the red color drain from her cheeks as she got more oxygen. When the crazed look in her eyes dissipated, I released her shoulders. She dropped into her chair, slumped over, and rubbed her eyes.

"I'm sorry, Dawson," she said, "I don't know what got into me."

"It's okay; we all get a little carried away sometimes. How about you go to the back room and nap for an hour or so, and when you get back, you can tell me what you've found so far."

She eyed me warily. "What if Chief Probst finds out?"

"He won't," I said, "Cathy called us about the case yesterday because Probst is out of the office for a few days. His secretary told me he's in a budget meeting with the city all week."

"I suppose if he's not here, then—" She yawned and stretched her arms above her head. "Just an hour, though."

"Right, just an hour to get you through the day."

Three hours later, I heard a commotion from the back room. The room wasn't much more than a storage closet, barely big enough for the small cot. The bed wasn't very comfortable, but when the officers at the station were pulling long hours and couldn't get home to a real bed, it was better than the floor. Chief Probst had tried repeatedly over the years to get rid of the cot, but it always reappeared a few days after he tried throwing it out. He finally declared that the cot was possessed by a ghost and that since he couldn't get rid of it, we were all banned from using it. We still did when necessary, but were careful not to let the Chief find out.

"Dammit, Falco, I said one hour!" Sophia yelled down the hall.

Everyone turned and looked at me. "What? She needed to sleep," I told them. When they all kept staring at me, I said, "You guys don't have to deal with her when she's being a bear because she's tired!"

A minute later, Sophia plopped down at her desk, a scowl on her face. Without a word, I handed her a fresh cup of coffee, doctored the way she liked it. I didn't say anything as she took her first few sips, but I could practically see the caffeine working its way into her bloodstream. When the scowl eased to a frown, it was safe to talk to her.

"How was your nap?"

"I told you one hour. Why did you let me sleep for three?"

"Because you needed it, Sophia," I said. "You can't function at 100% if you're too tired."

"Yeah, I suppose you're not wrong," she pouted.

"You can say *not wrong* all you want, but it still means you think I'm right," I teased.

She rolled her eyes, but a laugh escaped her. "What have you been working on?"

"Not too much, just wasting my time going through some of the most useless CCTV footage I've ever seen."

"No good shots of our perp?"

"No good shots of anything," I said. "Some of the cameras are pointed straight down the road. It catches all the license plates but doesn't help us much."

"And the others?"

"The others are either so dirty you can't make anything out, or trees completely block them."

"So, we still don't have a face to run through the databases?"

"Unfortunately, no. I've come up empty." It was my turn to rub my face in frustration. "Do you want to tell me what you've been up to all night?"

"I spent most of the night trying to get the search parameters right. I started with gender as female, height between 5' 5" and 5' 9", weight under 120 pounds, and age 25-35."

"You didn't get any hits with those?"

"There were fifty or so hits, but I ruled most of them out. Several had distinct tattoos that would've been impossible for our witnesses not to notice. Several others were in jail during the first two murders. Since I agree with your theory that this is a serial killer, I ruled them out."

"Tell me how you set your search values," I said. "Maybe if you tell me your thought process, I can help you figure out where else to look."

"I chose the height range based on the pictures of her side-by-side with

Grace and Callum. I added an inch on either side to account for shoes and Grace's hair."

"Okay, that sounds reasonable. How do you know the age is 25-35?"

"Based on the victims' ages. Grace was 22 and looking for a husband, so I doubt she would've been interested in someone younger and possibly less mature than her. But, according to her friend, Jill, she was smart about men, too. I don't picture her being interested in a much older man. She would've seen a man over 35 as creepy.

"Callum and Ling were both reported to be loners, so it stands to reason that they would fall into that same age range: not settling for young and dumb, not desperate enough for old and creepy."

"That makes sense. I don't think your age range is the problem."

"I think my problem is the weight. Women's weight is too big of a variable," she explained. "120 pounds on a tall woman looks completely different than 120 pounds on a short woman. Curvy, athletic, big-chested—it all looks different. And weight can fluctuate too much, too. The mugshots could be 50 pounds before weight gain or after weight loss. So, unless our suspect was arrested in the last six months and managed to maintain a stable weight, it's not likely to help."

"And you can't use hair length or color," I added, "Because that can be changed in a matter of hours."

"Right, that's why I didn't include that at all. I knew it was pointless."

"I'm going to play devil's advocate for a second," I said. "You're stressing out about not having the parameters set correctly when looking through mugshots in various criminal databases, right?"

"Right," Sophia answered skeptically.

"What proof do we have that she has a mugshot at all?" I asked.

Sophia stared at me. I could tell the gears in her brain were working hard. "You're saying that someone that has killed three people in relatively public places and left no evidence or DNA behind has never been arrested?"

"It's possible—"

"But not likely. Statistically, murderers get caught doing lesser crimes like burglary or killing animals and then escalate to killing people. They need practice to leave a crime scene with no evidence or witnesses."

"Statistically, yes, but not always. David Berkowitz didn't have a criminal record before becoming Son of Sam. And Dennis Rader had a few restraining orders taken out against him, but he was never arrested until they figured out that he was BTK. And that was years after his original crime spree."

"I see your point, but those are exceptions to the rule," she pointed out. "But if that's the case, if our suspect doesn't have a criminal record, how are we supposed to find her?"

"I think you need to go back to Barn Sour," I said.

"Why do I need to go back there?"

"No, not go back to the bar, but go back to your search." She looked at me like I had three heads, so I continued. "Traffic cameras. When we looked into the vehicles, we ignored the ones registered to women. Maybe you should look at those vehicles at Barn Sour the night Grace was murdered."

"Damn, that's a good idea," she said.

"I know, I'm full of them," I said smugly.

* * * *

At lunch, I hurried to the break room. Harper's chicken parmesan with homemade fettuccine alfredo was waiting in the fridge. I warmed it up, inhaling the delicious smell emanating from the microwave. I salivated as I walked back to my desk.

"Do you want any of this?" I asked Sophia.

"We both know you're only asking to be polite, but you don't want to share with me."

"So-o-o-o, you *don't* want any?" I clarified.

"No, Dawson, I don't. I want to find our murderer."

"Suit yourself," I quipped, twirling the noodles around my fork.

My phone rang as I finished the noodles. I was about to cut into the chicken, my knife and fork poised above the meat. I considered ignoring the call so I could enjoy my lunch for once. But who was I kidding? I was a detective first and a human second. Lunch would have to wait.

"Falco," I answered.

"Falco, it's Cathy. I'm done with the autopsy on our vic from the alley. I need you down here pronto to go over the results."

"Can it wait 15 minutes?" I asked, eyeing my lunch.

"Unfortunately, not today. I've got a rush job on an elderly woman whose family is certain she didn't die from her diagnosed congestive heart failure but was, in fact, murdered."

"All right, I'll be there in a few minutes." I turned to Sophia. "Let's go;

118

Cathy needs us."

"Can you handle this one autopsy by yourself, please? I need to get through as many of these DMV records as possible today."

I hesitated. I *could* go to the morgue alone, but I didn't *want* to. I couldn't tell Sophia that, though. Before stepping away from my desk, I looked sorrowfully at my lunch. I'd been looking forward to that chicken since Harper packed it last night after supper. She would be pissed if she found out I had wasted another perfect meal. So, I took it with me, eating it like a piece of pizza as I walked through the maze of hallways to the morgue.

It wasn't until I got outside the morgue doors and inhaled a whiff of chemicals that I regretted filling my stomach. I took a few deep breaths. Cathy would never forgive me if I threw up in her morgue, and she would never let me live it down. When my stomach settled, I went in. Cathy leaned too casually on the table where our victim was lying.

"It's about time," Cathy said. "What took you so long?"

"It's only been five minutes. What did you find?"

"The chopsticks did the trick," she said. "The first one went into the ear. It punctured through the eardrum and into the medulla, which controls the cardiovascular and respiratory systems. With that injury alone, he would have had difficulty breathing, his blood pressure would have skyrocketed, and he would have eventually died of lack of oxygen."

I grimaced, a phantom pain shooting through my ear.

"Don't worry, Falco; the second chopstick killed him shortly after." She pried Ling's eyelid open and pointed to the deformed eyeball. "Because of the upward angle of entry, the stick went into the frontal lobe, through his brain, and hit the inside of his skull on the other side. Your guy would've had to have some serious force behind that stab."

"Girl," I said.

"Huh?"

"Our girl. The murderer is a woman," I said, looking away from the creepy eye.

"You don't say?" Cathy seemed almost pleased. "It's about time a woman showed some spunk. And you still think all three are connected?"

"We are fairly certain they are, yes."

"Then you are looking for a woman with some serious rage issues. Blunt force trauma, hacking with a butcher knife, and now stabbing a guy *in the brain* with a chopstick?" She shook her head. "This girl is angry at someone or something."

"I know the drug screen for the other two came back negative. Did you get the same results on this guy?"

"This guy had low levels of Oxy in his system consistent with his prescription, but not enough to incapacitate him."

"The same with the alcohol levels in Grace and Callum. Did you find anything that might help us narrow down the suspect pool? A hair or bite mark?"

"Sorry, Falco, nothing like that."

"It's just another dead end, then," I said, defeated. "Will you send copies of the reports to Sophia and me?"

"Only if you get Harper to make me whatever it is you dripped on your tie." She pointed to my chest. "Is that red sauce? It must've been good."

I looked down, and sure enough, there was a red blob of marinara sauce on my tie. I swore and wiped it off. Could this day get any worse?

Where it all Began

Scotland holds a special place in my heart because it's the only thing I know about my heritage and where I came from. I was raised in foster care and never knew my biological parents. As most foster and adoptive children do, when I turned 19, I did a DNA test. I wasn't interested in finding my parents or any distant family. I was only interested in my ancestry and any medical concerns I may need to be aware of in the future. The results revealed that I was 75% Scottish. I was ecstatic.

Naturally, Scotland was my first destination when I graduated from culinary school. I planned to spend the summer sightseeing before returning to the US and starting my career. Life had different plans for me, though.

I ended up going to over a dozen Highland Games. These games are held nationwide and staggered by region, much like our county fairs. The games hosted dance competitions, sheepdog trials, cattle shows, and more. My favorite part, besides eating all the excellent traditional food, was the athletic competition. The hammer throw, tug-of-war, and caber toss were my favorites.

At my first event, I befriended a hammer thrower named Hamish and convinced him to teach me to throw. I felt a connection with Hamish, a camaraderie. I saw him at the next few shows, and he taught me how to do more of the events. I'll admit I wasn't very good at any of them. But I had fun and made some memories.

Hamish also introduced me to Mac, his boyfriend. I had seen Mac at competitions, too, but on a different team. I had never noticed so much as a yearning glance between them. They told me they kept their relationship quiet during competition season since they were on opposing teams. They didn't want to be accused of cheating or throwing a match, which seemed sensible. The three of us spent a lot of time together that summer, discussing our dreams and plans for the future.

As my time in Scotland drew to an end and I planned to go back to the United States, Hamish and Mac took me to a pub. There, Mac made me an offer that changed my life. His family, the McCullaghs, owned a farm and a popular restaurant in Skye. They raised all the animals whose meat they served at the restaurant. The McCullaghs were farm-to-table before it was cool. Mac told his family all about me, my new career as a chef, and how

how much I loved Scotland. He convinced them to let me live with them and work on the farm and in the restaurant. At that point, I'd never loved anyone as much as I loved Mac and Hamish.

Foster care taught me to figure things out on my own, make my own path, and rely on no one. Yet, here I was, being offered a fantastic opportunity by someone that owed me nothing. He saw something in me and extended me the kindness.

I started at the McCullagh farm a week later, leaving Mac and Hamish to finish the season without me. I was required to work on the farm first: shearing sheep, herding cattle, and gathering eggs. Then I was allowed to help butcher and process the meat. In two weeks, I learned more from them about cuts of meat and their uses than I learned in two years of culinary school.

When I "graduated" from the farm, I was allowed in the kitchen. I worked in awe as three generations of McCullagh women laughed, told stories, and sang old Scottish songs. All while they taught me the most authentic Scottish cuisine. We made sausage rolls, haggis, and my favorite, shepherd's pie. My stomach was always full that summer, but so was my soul.

In October, Mac and Hamish returned to the village, and we fell into our old rhythm. I was tempted to stay with them forever. I know I would've been welcomed by everyone. But I was itching to get out into the world and see what other adventures I could find. In November, I said my tearful goodbyes to the family, gave an extra-long hug to Mac and Hamish, and promised to visit again someday. I received an invitation to Mac and Hamish's wedding a few years later but couldn't attend.

Though Omaha has a reputable Scottish-Irish festival, I haven't been there in many years. Partially due to my demanding schedule as a restaurant owner, but also because it brings back a flood of memories. It makes me yearn to see my old friends. I want to take my husband there someday to show him the place where I began my journey around the world. I also need to show the McCullagh women that my shepherd's pie is now almost, but not quite, as good as theirs.

Shepherd's Pie

PREP TIME: 15 mins   COOK TIME: 50 mins
TOTAL TIME: 65 mins   SERVINGS: 4 servings

INGREDIENTS
- 1 teaspoon salt
- 3 large potatoes, peeled and quartered
- 8 tablespoons butter, divided
- 1 onion, chopped
- 1-2 cups mixed vegetables, usually diced carrots, corn, and peas
- 1½ pounds ground lamb
- ½ cup beef broth
- 1 teaspoon Worcestershire sauce

INSTRUCTIONS
- Boil potatoes until fork can easily pierce.
- Place potatoes in bowl with 4 tbsp butter and mash until desired consistency, seasoning to taste.
- In skillet on medium heat, sauté onions and vegetables in 4 tbsp butter for 6-10 minutes until warmed through.
- Add ground lamb to pan and cook until browned. Drain excess fat.
- Add broth and Worcestershire sauce to meat. Bring to simmer, then reduce heat. Cook uncovered for 10 minutes. Add more broth if needed.
- Scoop filling evenly into casserole dish.
- Spread potatoes over top. Use fork to rough up the surface so peaks brown.
- Bake at 400° for 30 minutes. Broil for 2-4 minutes for crispier potatoes.

Chapter 12
Sophia Leoni

I was so tired from work. Three bodies in ten days were more than double what we were used to. It would've been considered a slow week in Chicago, but it was a lot in Omaha. I'm not saying that's a bad thing. It's why I came here: to slow down, see fewer horrible things, and enjoy my life more.

So far, I have been doing the first two. There were fewer cases overall. Chief Probst didn't want his department to look like a bunch of bumbling idiots, so he sent us to a lot of training to keep our skills sharp. A large chunk of our caseload is gang-related and reasonably easy to close. The rest are the usual domestic violence gone too far, robbery gone wrong, or a hunter gone drunk. I had yet to see anything like the torture and mutilations that I saw routinely in Chicago.

We are now facing the first serial murderer in Nebraska since the 1950s. I'm finally convinced that the murders of Grace, Callum, and Ling are connected. Despite all the differences, I can't argue that Dawson was right from the start. We are looking for one despicable woman who kills at random for no apparent reason other than she enjoys killing.

This morning, Dawson and I spent hours reviewing the case, scrutinizing every detail, and trying to figure out our next move.

"We haven't talked about a motive yet," Dawson said.

"We decided they weren't robberies," I pointed out.

"Sure, we ruled that out. But we haven't figured out *why* she's killing."

"That's because we both know we don't need a motive for a conviction. Only police dramas need a motive to satisfy the viewer." I stared at him, "We know that sometimes, people do horrible things to other people just because they want to."

"So, these were crimes of opportunity. The victims were in the wrong place at the wrong time. The weapons were on-hand: a skillet from a cooking kit and chopsticks from a restaurant.

"Except the knife, which she brought with her into the Scottish festival."

"She was planning on murdering someone, even if she didn't know who," he said.

"Right," I agreed. "It's unlikely that she went in targeting Callum. He travels all over the country. It would be impossible for her to know that he would be at the festival."

"Grace was a regular at Barn Sour, but if our suspect didn't know her personally, she would've been gambling that Grace was there that night."

"And Ling just happened to be out walking," I said. "All our witnesses said he was a loner."

"You do know this is all bad news for us, right?" he said with a scowl.

"Why do you say that?"

"Because it means we may not be able to find her unless she kills again."

It was a sobering thought, and it's eating at me that we haven't been able to solve any of the crimes yet! Other than the realization that we are looking for a woman, we have nothing. I spent all day searching every system and database covering Nebraska and the surrounding states. Even going back through the DMV registrations for the vehicles we noted at Barn Sour proved a gigantic waste of time. The whole case was very frustrating.

When I got home, I was exhausted. I wanted to go to sleep, but my brain was still in overdrive. I stood at my front window and peered out at my new city. I lived downtown in a cute studio apartment. Even in the middle of Omaha, it was still quieter and calmer than where I grew up in Chicago. The city was calling to me tonight. It wanted me to leave my apartment and forget about work. I gave in to the call.

For the first time in months, I put a little effort into my appearance. I dabbed makeup on my face, doing my winged eyeliner the way I used to in college. I even curled my hair! Then, I dug into the back of my underwear drawer and pulled out my favorite lacy bra and panties, slipping them on. I wasn't wearing them in hopes that someone would see them. These were just for me, to make me feel feminine and sexy. I slid my best low-rise jeans up my hips and pulled on a low-cut, flowy shirt.

125

I walked the five blocks to Kings & Queens, my favorite club. Like all the buildings in this part of Omaha, the club was in a converted warehouse with ivy-covered brick outside and exposed brick inside. The atmosphere in the club was just what I needed tonight. The music was loud, and the rave lights flashed brightly in the dark. The large room smelled like sweat, alcohol, and lust. Gyrating bodies filled the dance floor. Men danced with men, and women danced with women, free to be themselves in Omaha's only gay club.

Since I moved to Nebraska, I've kept my sexuality a secret. It's not that I'm ashamed to be a lesbian. I came out to my dad and grandmother when I was still in high school. They supported me and encouraged me to attend pride parades. They also welcomed my few girlfriends into our home without question.

When I put in for the transfer to Omaha after my father died, my Chief brought me into her office and sat me down. She explained that Nebraska was still a fairly conservative state with old-fashioned beliefs. Not that it wasn't *safe* for homosexuals, but it could affect my life for the worse until I got established. She recommended I withhold personal information until I made friends and proved myself a good cop.

I took a few days to consider her offer but quickly realized she was right. Even though it was illegal to discriminate based on sexual orientation, bigots would find other ways to accomplish their goals. I didn't want an inconsequential thing like my sexuality to affect my work. Nor did I want to be the token "gay cop" in the Omaha PD.

I promised myself I would tell people once I was accepted into my unit. When that happened quicker than anticipated, I decided to wait until I had seen people's true colors and knew which ones could be trusted. When there were no problems, I figured I might as well wait until I found someone I wanted to date. Since I never found a woman I was interested in, I just kept quiet.

I haven't even told Dawson and Harper, and I was closer to them than anyone else here. I wasn't deliberately keeping it from them, but I knew they would be hurt when I finally told them. They would under-stand how big of a decision it is to come out to new people. I worried they would think it meant I didn't trust them. That was far from the truth, though. By the time I was ready to tell them, we had become such good friends that it seemed irrelevant. They would care for me whether I dated a woman or a wombat. So, why mention it?

"A fuzzy navel, please," I called to the bartender when I got to the front of the line.

While I waited for my drink, I scanned the room. I became acutely aware that there were a dozen women here that fit the description of our murderer. Many of the men would've been viable suspects, too. A curvy woman with long, wavy black hair—the opposite of our suspect—caught my eye. She smiled. I smiled back.

Maybe I'll let her see my panties, I thought.

When the bartender brought my drink, I held out my credit card. "It's been taken care of," she said, nodding to the end of the bar.

I looked, but the curvy woman wasn't there anymore. Several other women were standing at the end of the bar, but they were all turned away. I didn't know who to thank.

I took a sip of the fuzzy navel. It was sweet and a little tart. I could see why Grace liked it so much! I sucked down most of the drink, wanting to get a buzz going as quickly as possible. One of my favorite songs blasted through the room, so I headed for the dance floor. I pushed through the crowd until I found an open spot. I began to feel the music course through me, the bass like a heartbeat. I had complete freedom to be myself.

I wasn't worried about being seen at a gay bar. The only other gay person I knew in Omaha was Jean-Pierre. He'd told me several times that he wouldn't be caught dead sweating in a club lest it messed up his hair. All my friends and coworkers were in happy hetero relationships. Unless someone led a secret double life, which seemed too risqué for a Mid-westerner, I doubted I would run into them here.

I felt a hand on my waist and a supple body pressed gently against my back. I stiffened momentarily, but she started gently swaying, and I leaned back into her. My body fit perfectly with hers. We moved in unison for a few glorious minutes. As my hands wandered her body, I realized it wasn't the curvy woman. My soft hands ran up her thigh and around the small bump of her ass. Her soft lips nuzzled my neck and my ear.

When the song ended, I turned around to see my mystery partner. I gasped in shock and jumped away from her. "What are you doing here?" So much for not seeing any of my straight friends here.

"I needed a night away from you-know-who," she said.

"But why here?" I yelled as the next song started. "You know this is a gay bar, right?"

She gasped and covered her mouth with her hand, feigning shock. "I had no idea! I didn't notice all the couples were the same sex."

"But you aren't gay. You're married!"

"We all have our secrets."

"But you kissed my neck?" I said, touching the warm spot where her lips had been.

"Because you're a beautiful woman, and you deserve to be kissed. I'd like to kiss more of you."

She put her hand on my waist and pulled me close again. I didn't hesitate. We started moving together, stiffly at first, then blending into each other's bodies like we belonged together. I put my head on her shoulder and wrapped my arms around her, sliding my hands into her back pockets. She ran her hand up and down my back. When she pulled gently on my hair, I looked up at her. She kissed me so deeply I never wanted to come up for air.

She whispered, "Let's get out of here."

"We can't," I told her. "What if he finds out?"

"He won't," she assured me. "Even if he did, he would be so turned on. Trust me."

"This isn't a joke. I don't want to ruin things for you. Or for me."

"You won't. He'll never find out." She drew an X over her heart and said, "Cross my heart and hope to die."

I wasn't convinced. She cupped my cheek in her soft palm and looked into my eyes. I saw only sincerity reflected back at me. I nodded.

"Your place," she said. Not asked, said. She smothered my protest with a kiss.

I don't think I've ever walked so fast in my whole life. We didn't speak, but we held hands and stayed as close as we could to each other. My skin burned wherever she touched me, and my anticipation grew as I thought of all the places I wanted her to kiss me. When we got to my apartment, I opened the door and pulled her inside.

"Do you want a beer?" I asked.

I didn't wait for an answer before I opened the fridge and stuck my head and torso inside. I stood for a few seconds, deeply inhaling the cold air. She laid her hand on my back. I slowly withdrew from the fridge. She gently turned me around and lifted me gracefully onto the laminate counter. I was surprised by her strength, considering her lithe form. She brushed my hair from my face and ran her fingers softly down my arm. She kissed me gently.

Without warning, I was filled with so much desire for her that I lost all control. I pulled her to me and wrapped my legs around her, unwilling to let her go. We were so hungry for each other. I ran my fingers through her short hair and pulled her head back. I kissed and bit her neck, her earlobes, her lips. She moaned and worked her hands under my shirt and bra. She pinched my nipple, and I gasped in pleasure. She pulled me off the counter and stood behind me, her hands running up my back.

Suddenly, I flew forward and smacked the wall. Pain erupted in my head, and I felt a stabbing sensation in my chest. I stood for several seconds, trying to figure out what I had tripped on. But I could feel the warm spots on my back where her hands had been, just under my shoulder blades. Even a rookie detective could figure out that I had not tripped but had been pushed.

I stepped back from the wall, and the pressure in my chest released. I saw my rocking pizza blade. It was covered in red. I looked down at my chest and saw the blood flowing down my abdomen. I put my hand over the long wound, trying to hold it closed.

I turned to her, hoping to see concern on her face, hoping that my instinct was wrong. But her face showed nothing: no fear, no tears, no remorse. I slipped in the blood pooling at my feet and hit the wall again, narrowly missing the blade. I slid down the wall onto the cold, tile floor. She knelt in front of. me. I noticed her carefully place her foot away from the blood, ensuring there would be no forensic evidence linking her to my murder.

"Why?" I begged.

"You were getting too close."

Food and Adrenaline

My true passion in life is, obviously, cooking. Why else would I spend a decade traveling the world and learning the trade? My second passion is extreme sports. I love anything that gets my heart pumping: skydiving, bungee jumping, hang gliding. You name it, I've already done it, or I'm planning on doing it soon.

While in Greece, there was one person in particular that shared my love of both food and adventure: Kostos. He was an unlikely friend, a 70-year-old man still young at heart. He spent most of his life building his family's restaurant empire, including the one that had been in his family for five generations. He had a tanned, weathered face that never looked angry and a mustache that would put Burt Reynolds to shame.

He called me *engoni*, the Greek word for granddaughter. I never knew my grandparents, so I was honored he saw me as such. With his blessing, the whole family welcomed me with open arms. He always complimented my cooking and let me be privy to some of the family's secret recipes.

Outside of the kitchen, we talked a lot about all of the daredevil activities we had done. He confided that his family wouldn't allow him to do those things anymore because of his age. I asked him to show me all the places in the Greek Isles to seek a thrill. It was purely an accident that he fell into a skydiving harness or walked into a snorkel mask and fins! Completely unavoidable!

The weekend before I left Greece, Kostos took me scuba diving in Rhino Cave. It's a beautiful underwater cave system with stalactites and stalagmites that curved like a rhino horn. It was a magical final excursion with a man I could describe with the same word.

I will uphold my promise to Kostos and not reveal any of his family's secret recipes. Instead, I'll share the recipe for the *tiropitas* he loved so much that he served it every night in all his restaurants.

Greek Tiropitas

PREP TIME: 35 mins
TOTAL TIME: 50 mins

COOK TIME: 15 mins
SERVINGS: 4 servings

INGREDIENTS
- ½ pound feta cheese, crumbled
- ½ pound cottage cheese, small curd
- 3 eggs, beaten
- ½ teaspoon salt
- ½ pound fillo dough, thawed
- ½ pound unsalted butter, melted

INSTRUCTIONS
- Combine cheeses, eggs, and salt in bowl and stir until blended.
- Lay fillo dough on cutting board and brush with butter.
- Cut into long strips 2 inches wide.
- Place 1 teaspoon cheese mixture at one end of strip.
- Fold one corner horizontally to make a triangle (like a folded flag). Repeat for all strips, using all filling.
- Place triangles on baking pan lined with parchment paper.
- Brush remaining butter on top of triangles.
- Bake at 350° for 10-15 minutes until golden brown.

Chapter 13

Falco, get in here!" Chief Probst bellowed from his office. "Now!"

I scanned my desk and my memory, trying to think what I had done that he was angry about. I hadn't told off any VIPs or requested any expensive tests to be run by the lab. I hadn't even fallen behind in my paperwork this month! I wasn't sure what he was so mad about, but I took a deep breath and headed into his office.

"Chief, you wanted to see me?"

"Where's Leoni? She's late."

I glanced at my watch. Chief was right. It was already 9:30, and Sophia was always on time. "I'm not sure, Chief. I haven't gotten a call or text from her. I haven't heard from her all weekend, come to think of it. I'll go track her down right now."

Before I could escape, he said, "How did you not notice she wasn't here yet? You're the senior detective; it's your job to keep track of her."

"Apologies, Chief. I was reviewing the autopsy report on the Chan murder and hadn't realized the time. I'll call her right now."

"Tell her if she doesn't want to be here on time, she can take her ass back to Chicago and waste their time."

I literally bit my tongue to keep from replying. I returned to my desk, calling Sophia as I went. Chief Probst was out of line with that comment. It's not like Sophia is habitually late. He's just one of those old-school cops that hadn't forgiven the new-school cops for telling him he can't dis-criminate based on race or gender.

Sophia didn't answer when I called or reply to any texts. I could feel anxiety growing in me as each minute passed, as each text went unread. After 20 minutes of not hearing from her, I opened the Find a Friend app. Sophia called me a worry wart when I told her I wanted us to use it in case something happened while investigating a crime scene. She'd said she hadn't needed it in Chicago, so she didn't need it here. I showed her dozens of news articles of cops getting ambushed during traffic stops and not being found until it was too late. She only agreed when I promised it would only be used for work purposes and emergencies. This just happened to be both.

Strangely, the app pinged her location at her apartment. But if she was home, why wasn't she answering her phone? I considered radioing dispatch and having them send a patrol unit to check on her. When I thought of the wrath that she'd rain down on me for sending a uniform to her door, I decided it was better to go myself.

It took me fifteen minutes to get to her apartment building. It was a newer building in downtown Omaha with the cold, steel architecture that was so popular now. I grimaced at the building, hating the lack of character. But it wasn't my residence, and Sophia liked the gym and other amenities that the complex had.

The developers had thought of all the extra bells and whistles to make the apartments luxurious but had neglected to consider even the most basic security measures. No guards were posted in the lobby, no keypad for the main door, and no security cameras anywhere on the property.

"You're a cop. You know the importance of security," I'd chastised her on more than one occasion. "You've got to move to a safer place."

"Who exactly do you think is coming after me?" she'd questioned.

"Do you want me to go with the s*mall, pretty female* excuse or the *bitch cop that arrested me* excuse?"

"Aww, you think I'm pretty?" she'd teased. When I didn't laugh, she added, "I feel safe here. Safer than I ever felt in Chicago. I'll consider moving when my lease is up, but I'm not going to break my lease and lose my deposit just because you're paranoid."

I rode the elevator to her floor and wracked my knuckles furiously on her door. "Police, come out with your hands up!" I called. When she didn't answer, I knocked again and yelled, "Police, open the door!"

The door across the hall opened, and an older woman stepped into the hall. When I saw her terrified expression, I apologized. "I'm so sorry, ma'am. I didn't mean to startle you. It's just a little joke."

She huffed and slammed her door.

I called Sophia again and pressed my ear to the door. *I Shot the Sheriff* rang out. I glared at the door, annoyed that that was the song she chose as my ringtone. I'd never heard it before since I never called her when we were together. Then I glared because she was obviously home but still wasn't answering the door. Even during her worst hangover, she always replied, even if it was just one word. Not doing so at all set alarms off in my head.

"Sophia, I'm breaking in if you don't open this door in five seconds. I've got probable cause. 'Cause you're probably just doing this to be an ass, but it's not funny! One, two—five!"

I stepped away from the door and grunted as I kicked near the handle. The door flew inside with a deafening crack. I stepped inside but didn't see Sophia. I peeked into the small bathroom; she wasn't in there. The studio was empty.

"Sophia?" I called out. When I received no reply, I mumbled, "Where the hell are you?"

I saw her phone sitting on the kitchen counter. I tapped the screen. It lit up and I could see the notifications for my missed calls and unread texts. She hadn't checked her phone at all this morning. Her phone was usually glued to her hand. The ball of anxiety grew even more.

My eyes jumped to something shiny and silver hanging from the wall at the back of her kitchen bar, glinting with the sunshine streaming through the window. It was the long, curved-edge pizza blade that Sophia had mentioned to Harper and me last week at supper. It was caked in red pizza sauce. I guess she had been able to use it after all, but she could've cleaned it better.

A cold feeling ran over me, like a bucket of water dumped on my head. I looked back at the blade and realized it wasn't covered in sauce but in dried blood.

I ran to the kitchen. Sophia was sitting on the floor, her arms resting in her lap and her head tilted to one side. She could've been sleeping if her eyes had been shut. And if there wasn't a pool of blood surrounding her. I stepped forward, then stopped. She wasn't my friend now; she was a victim. I wasn't in my friend's apartment; I was at a crime scene. I had to preserve it. Sophia would understand.

I was careful not to touch anything as I left her apartment. In the hall, I called dispatch.

"This is Detective Dawson Falco of the Homicide Division, Badge #1106. I have an officer down at 8963 Kenesaw Ave. Apt 423." I was so calm I was scaring myself.

"Detective, do we need to send an ambulance?" the dispatcher asked.

"No, the officer is 10-45," I said, giving the police code for *deceased victim*.

"Detective, stay where you are; we have units on the way. They should be there in two minutes."

I hung up and slid down the wall. The edge of my vision blurred, and my hearing became muffled. I heard officers rush up the stairs. One tapped my shoulder and tried to get me to give a statement, but my brain wouldn't respond. It wasn't until Cathy arrived that I snapped out of my daze.

"Falco, I'm so sorry," she said, all traces of her usual dark humor gone.

"I'll show you—" I started, but she put a firm hand on my chest.

"It's a crime scene, and you're her partner. You know you can't go in there, Dawson." It was the first time she'd ever used my first name.

"Yes, she's *my* partner. I have a right to be in there," I said. "I have a right to make sure she's taken care of. She's-she's—"

"She's in good hands. We'll take good care of her." Cathy choked back her tears. "*I* will take care of her. You need to go back to HQ and talk to Probst."

I took out my car keys, but my hands shook so badly that I dropped them. Cathy handed the keys to a uniformed officer and instructed him to drive me back to the station. In the blink of an eye, we were there. The officer handed me my keys and tried to offer his condolences. I climbed out of the car, silencing him with the slamming door. I went straight to Chief Probst's office.

"What's the plan, Chief?" I asked. "How are we going to handle this?"

"You're not going to handle anything. You're going to go home," he said, more gently than I'd ever heard him speak. "You are relieved of duty while we process Leoni's crime scene. Mansfield and Parks will be assigned her case."

"Absolutely not," I yelled, "Those two wouldn't know a—"

"It's not up for debate, Falco." His familiar gruff voice was back. "You know you aren't allowed to investigate a murder you're so close to. And Mansfield and Parks are great detectives."

"I want updates," I demanded. "Every hour. I want to know what's happening and who the suspects are. I want to—"

"I don't give a rat's ass what you want, Falco. You're emotional. You'll botch the investigation, or worse, go on a vigilante rampage. I can't have either of those."

"But I'll—"

"You'll go home," he said, "You'll rest. And you'll stay out of our way and let us do our job."

"Check the other cases? This has to be related to the other three cases."

"We have no evidence right now to support that. But," Chief held up a hand to stop my protest, "If we find a reason to believe you are right, Mansfield and Parks will take over those other cases."

"That's horseshit!" I screamed. "Those are our cases!"

I choked on my own words. *Our.* They weren't *ours* anymore. They would be mine because Sophia isn't here to work them with me.

Without another word, I fled Chief Probst's office. I ran to my car, jumped in, and headed home. Clever Culinary was closed on Mondays, so Harper would still be at home. I had to tell her before the news broke. This would destroy her.

When was the last time she had seen Sophia? Was it the night she had come over for fajitas, and I'd ruined the evening? No, we had lunch at Clever Culinary after Callum's murder and talked to her about the weapons. Harper had been out having drinks with friends on Friday night. Was Sophia with her? Did they run into each other at a bar? Sophia had been dressed up, and her makeup was done, so she had gone out at some point this weekend.

I pulled into the garage and got out of my car. Harper's green truck was still there. I leaned against it and tried to gather my strength before entering the house. When I was ready, I pushed open the door. Bluegrass music was blaring from the sound system, and I could hear Harper moving around in the kitchen. I peeked around the corner and saw her smiling as she sang along to the music. I knew it would be the last time I'd see that smile for a long time. I wanted to soak it in for just a second. Then, I stepped into the kitchen, unable to put it off any longer.

Harper jumped when she saw me. "Whoa, honey, you scared me," she cried. "What are you doing home?"

I couldn't say anything. I just looked at Harper. Her smile vanished. She walked hesitantly around the island.

"Dawson, what's wrong?" she asked. "Did something happen at work? Did you get another bad case?"

I nodded my head, tears welling in my eyes. All I could manage was, "Sophia."

She put her hands over her mouth. "Wha-what happened to Sophia? Dawson, tell me what happened!"

I couldn't hold it together any longer. I started crying huge, wracking sobs that tore at my whole body and stole my breath. I cried like a teenage girl in a movie, ugly and heart-wrenching, but I didn't care. I'd just lost my partner and best friend, the most important person in my life, second only to Harper. My knees buckled. Somehow Harper caught me, and we sank to the floor, both of us crying now. She held me tight as I lay on the tile floor and mourned my friend.

Hours later, Harper convinced me to get off the floor and go to bed. I let her lead me to the bedroom, remove my clothes, and tuck me into bed like a child. But I knew I wouldn't sleep; my mind spun too fast. I was grateful when she crawled into bed next to me.

"What are you going to do now?" she whispered.

"I'm going to work on her case," I said matter-of-factly. "I'll talk to Cathy and get copies of all the reports. I'm going to go to the station and get all the files I have on the last three victims, and I'm going to nail this woman and put her ass in prison."

She furrowed her eyebrows. "Why do you think this is the same person that killed the other three?"

"It has to be. Who else would want to kill Sophia?" I shouted.

"Hey, I'm on your side, remember? I'm just trying to make sure you're thinking clearly before you do something you regret."

"The only thing I regret is not being there for her when she needed me."

"No. No, you aren't going to do that," Harper said sternly, grabbing my chin and forcing me to look at her. "You aren't going to do that 'I'm a man, and I should've protected her' bullshit. Sophia was a grown-ass woman, and she knew how to handle herself. She wore the same badge as you. You had no way of knowing that she would be attacked, so you had no way of knowing that you could've helped her. Sophia would be pissed if you took that guilt on your shoulders."

I continued to glare at her until I could accept that she was right. Sophia would be pissed. I couldn't feel guilty about something I couldn't change, but I could damn sure catch the one that did this.

* * * *

That night, I slipped out of bed while Harper was fast asleep and quietly left the house. I drove to the police station. It was quiet inside; only a few detectives were still working. They barely glanced up at me as I walked to my desk. As quickly as possible, I made copies of all the evidence for Grace, Callum, and Ling. I dug around on Mansfield and Parks' desks to find any documents they already had on Sophia's case. There wasn't much, but the investigation was early. I took pictures with my cell phone of the other murder weapons and other evidence. I grabbed the papers in a haphazard stack and hustled to the exit.

At the last second, I changed course and descended the basement stairs. The morgue was even more terrifying in the dark at 1:00 am. Light from the streetlamps came in through the narrow hopper windows, reflecting off the stainless-steel tables and cooler. It cast the room in an eerie blue glow. I felt a shiver crawl over my whole body.

I set my bootleg files on the autopsy table and stood before the cooler. From left to right in the middle row, I could read Cathy's bold, block lettering: G WHITMORE, C MCINTYRE, L CHAN. They were all still there. Grace and Callum's families had completed all the paperwork to ship their bodies across state lines, but they hadn't been released from police custody yet. We were still trying to find Ling's next of kin. His autopsy was done, but I hadn't read the report this morning before getting called into Chief Probst's office.

I looked at the fourth drawer: S LEONI. Cathy and her team would've spent most of the day processing the crime scene, scouring it more closely than the others, so her autopsy probably hadn't been done yet. Tomorrow, though. Tomorrow my friend would be cut up and searched and swabbed in hopes of finding anything that would lead us to the person that killed her.

I reached out and set my hand on the cold lever that would open Sophia's drawer. I wanted to open it and look at her beautiful face one more time. But it wouldn't be her face. It would be like looking at a mask of her face. It would be close but with none of the spark that made her Sophia.

The last time I saw her alive, she was smiling at a bad joke I'd made and flipping me the bird. I wanted that to be the last memory I had of her. Not this morning in her kitchen, and certainly not her lying on a steel slab. I dropped my hand.

I drove around Omaha for hours to clear my head. I rolled the windows down, letting the warm breeze wash over me. I cranked up the radio. The station played early 2000s music, which I'd loved as an angsty teen growing up in my lower middle-class neighborhood. I began singing along. My voice was terrible, but a catharsis settled on me with each song. I pulled into the garage after my favorite Blink-182 song finished.

Harper was still asleep when I climbed back into bed. I pulled her to me, vowing to never let her go and to never stop protecting her.

A Gift for Sophia

This recipe is a late entry due to a tragedy in our family. My husband, Dawson, is a detective with the Omaha Police Department. His wonderful partner, Sophia, was recently killed in the line of duty. Sophia and I had grown very close in the year that they worked together. We were true friends.

Sophia moved to Nebraska from Chicago. She was born there and raised by her father, a retired detective. After her mother's passing in 2000, Sophia's grandmother moved in to help raise her. She began her career as a uniform patrol cop ten years ago and quickly moved up the ranks to become one of the youngest detectives in Chicago Police Department history. After her father's death 18 months ago, Sophia decided she needed a change of scenery and a slower pace in life. Nebraska fit the bill.

Since she moved here alone and had no family waiting, I felt an instant kinship with her. Growing up in foster care, I understood how lonely and scary it could be to start over in a new place. So, I invited her to our house and did my best to make her feel right at home.

Before the end of the night, Dawson was all but forgotten as we talked about her life in Chicago and my travels abroad. It felt like we'd known each other forever. We even began to see each other without my husband present. He was relieved that there was no jealousy between us. He was even happier that he didn't have to go shopping with me anymore.

At every dinner since, we reminisced about our childhoods. Sophia wasn't much of a cook, despite her many cooking lessons with her grandma. But she still valued that time spent with her. She confided that the one thing her grandmother was never able to perfect was the Chicago Deep Dish Pizza. Just the week before she died, Sophia asked me to try making her a pizza that would be as good as any pie in Chicago. I promised her I would do just that the next time we got together.

When he told me our dear Sophia had been taken from us, I felt like my heart had been cut with a blade. We are both still grieving this loss and probably will forever. In honor of the promise I never got to fulfill, I'm including a simplified deep-dish pizza recipe I hoped one day would bring a slice of home to Nebraska for Sophia.

Chicago Deep Dish Pizza

PREP TIME: 8 mins   COOK TIME: 30 mins
TOTAL TIME: 40 mins   SERVINGS: 6 servings

INGREDIENTS
- 1 teaspoon oil
- 1 pound pizza dough (premade or use homemade dough recipe of choice)
- 1½ cups mozzarella, shredded
- ⅓ pound Italian sausage
- ⅓ cup pepperoni, diced
- ²/₃ cups pizza sauce (premade or homemade recipe of choice)
- ½ cup parmesan cheese, grated
- Other assorted toppings

INSTRUCTIONS
- Preheat oven to 425°
- Lightly oil bottom (not sides) of 9-inch cake pan.
- Press dough into the bottom and up sides of pan.
- Sprinkle 1 cup mozzarella cheese and spread evenly.
- Layer meat and other toppings, repeating as necessary to fill just below top of pan.
- Spread pizza sauce evenly over toppings.
- Top with remaining mozzarella and parmesan cheese.
- Bake for 30-35 minutes or until dough is golden brown.

Chapter 14

Cathy called me on Tuesday evening to tell me what she found during Sophia's autopsy.

"You didn't hear any of this from me, Falco," she warned. "I could lose my job and my license for telling you information on a case that isn't yours."

"I know, and I appreciate you doing this," I said. "But I have to know what you found."

Cathy sighed into the phone. "She died from blood loss due to the knife wound in her chest. She was pushed into the blade hanging on the wall. It's possible she tripped, but as deep as the knife went, a lot of force was used. That tells me your suspect pushed her from behind."

"Do you have a definitive date of death?"

"Sometime between Friday night and Saturday morning. I can't tell any closer than that with body temperature. Hopefully, the detectives on the case can get cell phone records or security footage from her apartment that'll give additional clues to when she was last seen alive."

I scoffed. "That apartment complex doesn't have any security cameras. I told Sophia months ago she needed to move somewhere more secure, but she wouldn't listen. She just—"

"Do you really think this is the best time for an *I told you so*, Falco?" Cathy spat. "She's dead. Sophia's dead, and it sucks. But blaming her for living in an apartment complex with no security cameras isn't going to bring her back!"

I was stunned into silence. I could tell Cathy was trying to choke back tears. In my grief, I forgot other people love Sophia, too. Other people are sad she's gone.

"I'm sorry, Cathy, I didn't mean it like that. I just—" I stopped, thinking of

141

the right thing to say. "I just miss her. And I want to get this woman who thinks she can kill whenever she wants and get away with it."

"So, you think this is connected to the other three cases?" Cathy asked.

"I do. It has to be. Did you find anything linking them?"

"Only the toxicology results. They were the same as the other three. Sophia had no drugs in her system, prescription or otherwise. We did find alcohol in her system, though."

"She must have gone out somewhere," I said. "She never dressed up or put on makeup unless it was for a special occasion. She had makeup on and her hair was curled when I found her. If she had alcohol in her system, she must have gone out somewhere for drinks."

"Should I tell Mansfield and Parks about your theory?" Cathy asked. "They'll be down here soon to go over these results."

"Yes, they need to know. I doubt they'll follow up on it, though," I said.

"Don't do anything stupid, Falco," Cathy said sternly, "You can't help Sophia if Chief Probst arrests you for interfering with an investigation."

"I don't need a lecture, Cathy," I fumed, "I just need you to email me your results."

For the next few days, I thought about nothing but Sophia's murder and the other three connected cases. I had taken over the dining room table, obsessively reading and rereading all the paperwork. I had to find the one missing clue that would give me the grand reveal worthy of a TV police procedural.

On Wednesday, Harper handed me a piece of paper. I glanced at it and read, *In Honor of Sophia* at the top. It was an intro for a recipe.

"What the hell is this?" I snarled at Harper.

"It's a tribute, I suppose," Harper replied. "It's the only way I know to honor Sophia."

"I don't have time to read this," I said, tossing it aside.

Harper snatched it back up and began reading it out loud. I could barely listen to her. *"We are both still grieving this loss and probably will forever. In honor of the promise I never got to fulfill, I'm including a simplified deep-dish pizza recipe I hoped one day would bring a slice of home to Nebraska for Sophia."*

She slammed the paper onto the table like she was making some sort of point. I slowly turned to look at Harper. She expected me to be misty-eyed about the intro. But I was furious!

"How dare you write that!" I yelled. "How dare you use that recipe!"

"What's wrong with that recipe?" she asked, legitimately confused.

I picked up a picture from the table and held it in front of Harper. "This is what's wrong!"

The picture was of Sophia's autopsy. It showed her naked torso with the laceration from her left breast, across her abdomen, to just below her ribcage on the right. The picture didn't show the lacerated organs or the amount of blood she lost before she slowly and painfully died. Harper gasped and turned away.

"The woman who attacked her pushed her into the pizza blade she bought specifically for deep-dish pizza. Don't you remember how excited she was about it? And now she'll never get to try it."

Harper's face was white. "I'm sorry. I didn't think of that," she said. "But I don't think Sophia would be upset about it."

"I guess we'll never know," I spat.

For the first time in the five years we had been together, I slept on the couch. I barely spoke to Harper for the next three days. I grunted when necessary but didn't speak to her or look her in the eye. I didn't eat, didn't shower or shave, and barely slept. I was simultaneously too tired to sleep and so tired I was unable to think of new ideas to help Sophia.

When Harper came home to check on me Sunday afternoon, she gave me some tough love.

"I'm not living with a smelly pig!" she yelled. "Take a shower."

"I don't have time for that, Harper," I yelled.

She glared at me. "I'm not asking. Shower, or get out of our house."

We knew I would never leave, so I trudged to the bathroom. I stood in the water, turning the knob to make it hotter and hotter. When it was almost scalding, Harper joined me. Usually, I would've been turned on. I would've pinned her against the wall and ravaged her until we needed another shower. But she barely got my attention now. She massaged my scalp with her fingertips as she washed my hair, then scrubbed my body with a loofah. I felt the weight of the past few weeks release and wash down the drain with the soap suds.

"You're coming to the restaurant with me," she said.

"No, I've got work to do."

"No, you've got a career-ending obstruction of justice case on the dining room table," she corrected.

"I'm not leaving work here while I sit at your restaurant and play on my phone all night."

She thought briefly before offering, "You can bring everything to the restaurant as long as you keep all the pictures put away until we close. And you have to eat something."

"I'm not hungry," I said.

"You may not think so, but you haven't eaten in almost a week. You need protein to keep up your strength for this—" Harper waved her hand dismissively at the files on the table, "—vigilante crusade."

Right on cue, my stomach growled obscenely. I could see her resisting the urge to smirk at me. "Fine, I'll go. I'll meet you there."

"If your ass isn't at a table in 30 minutes, I'm calling Chief Probst and telling him what you've been up to." She turned on her heel and stalked out the door.

Thirty-*one* minutes later, I walked into Clever Culinary. I was a minute late to show her she didn't have complete control over me. I dropped my briefcase on a family-sized table and glared at her. She was standing behind the bar with her cell phone in hand, poised to call Chief Probst. Jean-Pierre dropped a plate of chicken wings at the table a few minutes later.

"She told me *not* to talk to you," Jean-Pierre whispered, "But I wanted to tell you how sad I am about Sophia. She was a *wonderful* woman."

I grunted at him and dug into my plate. No one bothered me again.

I continued working until after the dinner rush. After closing, Jean-Pierre turned off the lights behind the bar. The kitchen staff left by 10:00, and the restaurant became eerily quiet. Harper hadn't come to tell me she was leaving, so I sat there, alone and confused, continuing my work.

I pulled out the pictures of the crime scenes and autopsies. I'd kept them in my briefcase like Harper had asked, but now I added them to the top of the clutter. I paced around the table, trying to see the evidence from a different angle. I knew there was something here that I was missing, something that would tie all four cases together and expose the murderer.

Harper pushed through the kitchen door and stood across the table from me. "Honey, I think it's time to put these away," Harper said softly.

"No, I have to figure this out," I said. "I have to solve it."

"No. No, you don't, Dawson," she urged. "Mansfield and Parks have been—"

"Those idiots don't give a shit about Sophia." I glared at her. "They won't work hard enough to—"

"Yes, they will. Deep down, you know they will. Cops always take care of their own. They won't let him get away."

144

"*Her*," I corrected, "Won't let *her* get away. But there's something I'm missing! Something that's staring me in the face that connects them all!"

"If there is, Mansfield and Parks will find it."

I sat down in a chair and put my head in my hands. My anger was changing to desperation. "No, they won't. It's something about these cases. Something.... familiar."

"What do you mean?" Harper asked, still infuriatingly calm.

"It's almost like déjà vu. There's something about the victims and the weapons that I know I've seen before. I've got a picture in my head, but I don't know where the picture came from. When I figure it out, though, everything will come together.

"It hit me when Ling was killed with chopsticks—a Chinese man killed by a Chinese utensil after eating Chinese food. And you said yourself that most Southern cooking is done in a cast iron skillet. Grace was from the South. And Sophia was killed with the pizza blade she wanted to use for her Chicago pizza!"

Harper flinched. "I see the connection between the first two, but how does Sophia's murder fit in?"

"She's Italian! Pizza is from Italy!"

Harper still looked confused, and I screamed in frustration. She sank into a seat, scared. My heart fluttered. I went to her and sat beside her, taking her hands in mine. Tears welled as I said, "I'm so sorry, Harper. I didn't mean to scare you. I just... I just can't..."

Harper stared at me. Her fear turned to sadness and then to something else I didn't quite recognize. Acceptance? Defeat? I couldn't worry about her right now, though. She reached out and gently touched my cheek with her soft hand. Without a word, she left the dining room.

I picked up each victim's photo and set it on the pile. Then I grabbed the pictures of the murder weapons and set them by the corresponding victim. Like a madman, I started muttering, "Southern, skillet; Scottish, cleaver; Chinese, chopsticks; Italian, pizza blade," like a mantra.

I was so frustrated that I had to stand up and pace the restaurant, mumbling and cursing in cadence. I caught sight of myself in the glass of one of the pictures hanging on the wall. I stared at my reflection, not recognizing the unkempt man staring back at me. Then my eyes refocused on the picture: It was a Chicago deep-dish pizza. The pizza was served on an elevated silver stand. The stand sat on a red-and-white checkered tablecloth. On the tablecloth lay a clean, curved pizza blade—just like the one that had killed Sophia!

I finally recognized the pictures in my head as the pictures on the wall of Clever Culinary. Near the bar was a picture of the traditional Southern dish, a perfect chicken fried steak with country gravy, served in a clean cast iron skillet. By the front door, Chinese dumplings sat on a bed of fried rice. A set of chopsticks crossed over the dish.

Across the room was a shepherd's pie, topped with a perfect cloud of mashed potatoes. In the picture, the pie was still in the white casserole dish, with a rectangular butcher's cleaver sitting next to it. I had looked right at it the day Sophia and I came in to ask Harper about the weapons. I'd seen it and not put the clues together.

Thoughts flooded my brain. I had been right. All of the victims had been killed by items commonly found in kitchens. The weapon and the food in the pictures were specific to each victim's heritage. Was it a coincidence that Harper had the corresponding pictures in her restaurant?

That's when the last piece of the puzzle fell into place. I raced back to the table and snatched my briefcase from where I'd dropped it on the floor. I found the intros to Harper's recipes, the ones I had barely been able to finish in the last few weeks. I thumbed through them, pulling out the ones that proved that I hadn't been crazy all along.

The intro story from Harper's time in Scotland was about a red-headed gay man she met at a Scottish festival. The recipe that followed the story was for shepherd's pie. The man she met in China was shy, and they met because of the rains during the monsoon season. The recipe was for fried rice. I checked the copy of the order slip from Miss Yang's and saw fried rice listed. And I remembered reading about the southern woman that took her dancing before the recipe for chicken fried steak.

The description of our suspect matched, too. Harper was tall for a woman but would be considered short if disguised as a man. All the witnesses said there was no facial hair, typical for a woman. I remembered Mrs. Finnigan's hand gestures when she told us Callum's friend was straight or Miss Yang saying Ling's friend didn't have good hips for having babies. Sophia had even joked that Harper could pass as a man.

Cass. All the witnesses claimed the suspect's name was Cass—like Harper Cassidy. When we got married, Harper didn't want to take my last name. I had no problem with it; taking the husband's last name is outdated. She had already started building her career with her maiden name, Cassidy, so it made sense for her to keep it. Her restaurant was even derived from her last name. *Cassidy*, in Irish, often translates to *clever*, hence her restaurant's name, Clever Culinary. I never thought that she would use it as her alias for murder.

"No, it can't be her," I whispered as I continued to pace the restaurant. "She's a good person. She's my wife. I know everything about her."

I looked to the kitchen, deciding whether or not to confront her. Then another idea crossed my mind that might help prove me wrong. *The dates, I should check the dates. If she was with me the nights of the murders, then I'll be her alibi. If I can prove it's not her, I'll let the case go. I'll let Mansfield and Parks take over. Sophia would understand.*

I pulled my phone out and checked the dates. The Saturday that Grace was murdered, Harper had been in North Platte at a cooking competition. She'd driven all night to get back in time for her party at the restaurant Sunday afternoon. I quickly calculated the drive time and realized that had Harper left the competition when she claimed and driven straight home, she should've been home before midnight. She didn't get home until early in the morning, though. Even if she had stopped for food, gas, and a nap, several hours were still unaccounted for. She also would have had her competition cooking kit in the back of her truck, which gave her access to the skillet.

She couldn't have been at the Scottish-Irish Festival the night Callum was murdered, though. She'd gotten called into the restaurant because her sous chef called in sick. She'd canceled date night because of it. I remember the French toast the following day to make up for it. Then I flashed to the week after when I had teased Jean-Pierre for keeping her at work. *It's been months since Harper's had to cancel date night*, he had said. I thought he had his days mixed up, but maybe not. If she wasn't at the restaurant or with me, she easily could've gone to the Scottish-Irish Festival. She would've had her truck there that night, too. It was reasonable to assume that the knife found in Callum's chest had been removed from her cooking kit.

Ling was murdered the Wednesday between Grace and Callum. We knew the day because of the wet ground under his decaying body. I'd known the last time it had rained—the night I had come home to find Harper naked in the laundry room. We'd had sex during the spin cycle. Harper said she was washing her work clothes, but was she actually washing the clothes she wore when she stabbed Ling with the chopsticks?

The night Sophia died, Harper had been out with friends. I didn't even

147

know which friends because I never asked. I trusted Harper and never worried she was out with another man, so I never asked for details about who she was with or where she was going. On Saturday, when I'd asked what she had done with her friends, she'd just said dancing.

Anger burned in my gut, rising until it came out of me in a roar. I turned to the table and swept everything onto the floor. I collapsed on the ground and began to cry. My life was falling to pieces around me, and there was nothing I could do to stop it.

I heard a noise from the kitchen and was jolted back to reality. There was a murderer close. Harper was in the back. The noise sounded like pots banging together, but it could be anything. She had an entire kitchen full of weapons, and she had shown she knew how to use them.

I rose and drew my service weapon from my briefcase. I stood outside the swinging kitchen door and peeked through the round porthole window. I couldn't see anyone, but I could hear someone moving around. I pushed through the door, clearing left and right. I moved around the kitchen silently, clearing the pantry, the freezer, and the employee bathroom. More noise came from the dishwashing room, and I moved with my back along the wall. There was someone in there. I whipped around the corner and leveled my pistol on— Jean-Pierre.

Jean-Pierre let out the most high-pitched scream I'd ever heard. The pans he'd been holding clanged onto the floor, echoing in the small space. He held his hands up and screamed, "Don't shoot! Don't shoot!"

I lowered my weapon and whispered, "Jean-Pierre, where is Harper?"

"I-I-I don't know," he stammered. "She left through the back door fifteen minutes ago."

"Did she say where she was going?" I hissed.

"N-n-no. I thought she was taking out the trash, but I heard her truck start."

I left the kitchen through the back door to the alley. Harper's little truck— with the kitchen kit that was one skillet and one knife short—was gone.

Chapter 15

I ran through the restaurant, yelling at Jean-Pierre to call me if he heard from Harper. I jumped in my car and raced home, blue-and-reds flashing. It was the only place I could think of to look for her. Hopefully, she was stupid enough to go home and pack before fleeing, and I could catch her there. I considered calling for backup but needed to deal with this alone. I wanted to know what happened before I involved anyone else. Secretly, I was hoping she could explain everything away, and we would never have to tell anyone.

I jumped the curb in front of my house and slammed on the brakes. I stopped in front of both garage doors. If Harper had pulled her truck into the garage, I wanted to keep her from leaving. I didn't know if she would attack me, but I had to assume she would. If she could kill Sophia, I didn't think I would be off limits. I entered the house through the front door, where I could start clearing rooms. I noticed the bedroom light was on and made my way quietly there. I cleared the en suite bathroom and both closets. She was gone.

I sat down on the bed, frustrated and defeated. I had finally caught on, finally found our murderer, and I let her slip through my fingers. I pulled my cell phone from my pocket. It was a long shot, but I had to try calling her. I had to talk to her and make her tell me that I was wrong, that she didn't murder those people. Didn't murder Sophia.

"Hello, Dawson," Harper said, her voice casual.

"Where are you?" I asked.

"Don't worry, Dawson, I'm safe."

"It wasn't you, was it? Please, tell me it wasn't you?" I begged.

"I'm not sure what you mean."

I could hear the background noise of her driving, cars whipping by her on the road. She was on the move, but I didn't know where to.

"Don't play games with me, Harper. Did you kill those people?"

She paused for a second, then said, "Yes."

"Yes? That's it? That's all you have to say?"

"Do you want an explanation?"

"You're damn right I do! How could you do that, Harper? *Why* would you do that?"

"You won't like the answer, Dawson."

"Tell me anyway. You owe me that much."

She sighed loudly on the phone. "Dawson, I killed those people because I wanted to. I saw my opportunity with Callum, Grace, and Ling, and I took it. No evil plan, no manifesto, none of that. I just wanted to, and I could, so I did."

"What about Sophia? Why did you kill Sophia?" I begged her.

"Because she was too close to figuring out the truth. And if she figured it out, she would have to tell you. If she did, your duty as a cop would override your duty as a husband. It would override your love for me. And I didn't want to lose you."

"Then why are you running?"

"You figured it out. I have been trying all week to get you to let go of the case and hand it over to Mansfield and Parks. But you wouldn't stop! I could tell you were on the edge of piecing it together. There was nothing I could've done to stop it."

"Then why didn't you just kill me like you killed Sophia?"

"Because I love you!" Her voice cracked. "With my whole heart, I love you."

"Not enough to stop you from killing people," I snapped.

"That's not true, though. I stopped when we met."

I was thinking a million thoughts. "You stopped? You mean you've done this before?"

"Of course I have," she sounded insulted. "You know, first-time criminals don't leave clean crime scenes. There was no physical evidence because I've had practice. Even on the day I met you, I was scouting out a victim."

"Who?" I demanded. "Tell me who it was, Harper. A family out there doesn't know what happened to their loved one. Tell me who you killed!"

"I didn't kill anyone that day, Dawson. It happens to be the only time I decided to let someone go."

"Why?"

"Because my target... was you."

"Me?" I ran my hands through my hair, having trouble understanding.

"Yes. I saw you in the crowd at that cook-off long before you saw me. I knew I wanted to kill someone that day, and you were my choice."

"But we'd never met before," I said. "How did you plan to kill me when it was a coincidence that I was there?"

"I never have a solid plan, Dawson. When I feel like I want to kill someone, I make it happen. I just go with the flow and make do with what is available. I caught your eye on purpose so you would talk to me, and I could figure out how to get you alone. But after talking to you for a few minutes, I decided I didn't want you to die. Not at that point, anyway."

"So, you met me and decided to take five years off your part-time hobby as a murderer?"

"Not quite." She took a deep breath, deciding how much to tell me. "I took two years off, but when we were on our honeymoon, I had a moment of weakness. I was so excited to start my new life with you, but part of me felt like I missed my *last kill*. You know how smokers say quitting is easier if they know their last cigarette is the last? I felt that, too. You were supposed to die, but I changed the plan. I'm glad I did, but I wanted my last kill. I found a good one on our honeymoon."

"Who was it?" I asked.

"Does it matter, Dawson?"

"Yes, it matters to me."

"I'm sorry, Dawson, but I'm not going to give you that information."

"Doesn't matter," I said defiantly, "I'll figure it out. Was there anyone else?"

"No, there was no one else. Life was good for me. Things were going well with my restaurant and with us, so I didn't feel the need. But I was so stressed over the cookbook, and I needed to calm my nerves."

"Stressed?" I asked incredulously. "You're blaming the murders on stress?"

"Some people go to the gym, others the gun range. There's no difference."

"There absolutely is a difference, Harper!" I yelled. "People died! You killed people!"

"I see your point, but I stand by it," she said defiantly.

"How many, Harper?" I begged. "Tell me how many there are?"

"How many recipes are there?" she asked.

Realization dawned on me. "All of those intros you wanted me to read were your victims? All of them?"

"Yes, Dawson. All of them." She paused a second before saying, "Grace was supposed to be the only one. I felt the need to kill building inside of me for months, and that night everything aligned so nicely that I had to act. It's not often that I have a night with no one to vouch for my whereabouts while also having a pretty good alibi. And I did miss dancing. Meeting Grace was just luck, and the rest fell into place."

"That girl did nothing to deserve what you did to her," I snapped.

"Of course, she didn't *deserve* it," she said, "None of them deserved it. You don't seem to realize that Callum, Ling, and Sophia's deaths are on your hands."

"My-my hands? How the hell are their deaths on *my* hands."

"Think of the timeline, Detective," she urged angrily. "Grace died first, then who?"

"Ling," I said. "We didn't find him for a week, but you murdered him before Callum."

"I killed Ling on Wednesday after I found your little stash of unread intros in your nightstand. You worked late that night so I couldn't yell at you. I decided to take a walk in the rain. Ling found me. He was the one that suggested getting Chinese takeout. He was so busy trying not to freak out about being near a woman that he didn't see me grab those extra chopsticks and stick them in my belt." She drew a breath, "You see, if you would've read the intros like you had promised, Ling would still be alive."

"But you didn't find those for another week, Harper! That night I came home and you were mad wasn't for another week!"

"I felt better after killing Ling, so I decided to put them back in your drawer and not mention it to you. All week, I dropped hints that I knew you hadn't read them and hoped you would do your part. But you didn't. Even after you made an ass out of yourself at supper with Sophia, you still didn't read them! Then you dared to come into my restaurant and distract me from my writing. When I got home, I checked your stash and saw it hadn't been touched. I was too far behind to go out and find someone else to take my anger out on, so I took it out on you."

"And Callum?" I asked.

"The night Callum died we were supposed to have a date night. And where were you going to take me?"

152

"To Barn Sour," I replied. "You told me you wanted to go dancing."

"No, I didn't tell you that. You read that in Grace's intro. It was the one thing you remembered, and you applied it so poorly! I couldn't go back to Barn Sour the week after I killed Grace there! That bartender got a good look at me, and I don't think any amount of makeup would've fooled him."

"What does that have to do with Callum?"

"I had to ditch you for the night. I told you I had to go to work. I could've, too, but I was so furious with you that I would've been a liability in the kitchen. I decided to go to the festival instead. I'd been to the Highland Games before and thought it would be fun. Everything that happened with Callum was just the luck of the draw for both of us."

"Don't try to pull that bullshit with me, Harper. You took a butcher knife with you into the venue! You knew you were going to kill someone that night."

"I didn't *know* it, but I was prepared just in case," she said. "Regardless, if you would have just read the intros like you promised months ago, all those people would still be alive."

"You are a grown-ass woman, Harper. I won't let you pretend like these murders are anyone's fault but your own."

"And you're a grown-ass man that will have to come to terms with the fact that Sophia died because you are a bad husband *and* a bad detective."

"What...How do...I'm not..." I couldn't find the words.

"You're a bad husband because you promised to read the intros, but you didn't, Dawson. We've already established that," she huffed. "You're a bad detective because when you did finally read a few of them, you didn't see the similarities. It was all there in front of you. If you had just paid attention to the details, you might've caught on to Grace and Callum. Hell, I even gave you Ling's before you found the body! If you had just done what you promised and read the damn things, you could've put it all together. You would've caught me before I had to kill Sophia."

"She was your friend, Harper. How could you kill your friend?"

"Yes, that did make it a little harder. The rest were all acquaintances or people I had just met. For the cookbook, I exaggerate my relationship with them because it's better for sales. No one wants to hear about someone you barely know influencing your life."

"I'm going to find you, Harper. You're even stupid and arrogant enough to leave a printed log of your crimes."

"Oh, Dawson," she said like she was talking to a toddler, "you'll never be able to pin any murders on me, no matter how hard you try."

"I don't know, Harper," I growled, "I'm a pretty damn good detective."

"Didn't we just discuss how untrue that is?" she asked incredulously. "Besides, Dawson, you know I changed the details in the stories. I'm not dumb enough to name my victims. I did it for their protection. Well, mostly for *my* protection, but a little for them."

"I'll catch you, Harper. I swear I'll spend the rest of my life hunting you down."

"I don't doubt that. Your tenacity is just one of the things I love about you." She paused again. "I have to go now, Dawson. It's time for me to start over again. Just know that I'll always love you—"

"Wait, Harper, don't—"

"—cross my heart. Goodbye."

Chapter 16
Four Years Later

I took a seat in the little café. Everyone in the small village of Dingle, County Kerry, said this café sells the best pastries in all of Ireland. When I saw that the café was nearly full, I knew they were right. The small shop only had ten tables, and most were full. Couples, a group of friends, and even some singles were enjoying various treats. The shop assistant came to my table.

"What can I get for you, love," the young woman said in her beautiful lilt.

"There is so much to try," I said, smiling at her. "What would you recommend?"

"Our whiskey bread pudding is our top seller. It's what my family gets for all of our special occasions."

"I'll have one of those then."

When she had gone to the kitchen, I turned my chair to take in the full view of the beautiful Dingle Harbor. Fishing boats cruised slowly through the waters, returning with their day's catch. Seagulls filled the sky, daringly diving at the boats in hopes of stealing their supper.

The air was quite chilly, but nothing like the cold in Nebraska in October. It was a gamble to come to Ireland after the tourist season. I knew the weather wouldn't be great, but it was worth it. I was glad to leave Nebraska for this much-needed vacation. It had been almost seven years since I'd last taken a real vacation: my honeymoon with Harper.

My stomach clenched at the thought of her. She destroyed my life when she left. The restaurant still needed to be run, and the bills and staff still needed to be paid, but I had no idea what I was doing. The press coverage of the crimes and Harper's involvement didn't help, either. First, the staff and I were ridiculed for not realizing sooner that she was the murderer. Then, the rumors of Harper using her victims' flesh in the dishes started. Jean-Pierre tried to stand tall and become the restaurant's leader, but the damage was already done. The dining room was never full again. Even the regular customers stopped coming in. Within two months, I decided to close the doors of Clever Culinary.

I was suspended from the OPD Homicide Division pending an investigation into Harper. Even though they could find no evidence linking me to her crimes and I was reinstated as a detective, I couldn't do the job anymore. I knew I couldn't think objectively about any case because I would always try to connect Harper to it.

I transferred to the Tecumseh State Correctional Institute in Tecumseh, Nebraska. I was the lead investigator on the gang task force. It required long hours and thorough investigations, which didn't give me any time or energy to do anything but work. I'd go home to my one-bedroom apartment, grab a beer, and try not to think about Harper.

Until the day I got a package in the mail, that is. It had been sent to my Omaha address—the house I had shared with Harper—then forwarded to my new apartment. I tore open the box and pulled the book from it. *Travel on a Full Stomach: An Around-the-World Journey of Food and Friends*. It was Harper's cookbook, full of stories of people she had murdered.

I sat down that night and read it from cover to cover. There were over 30 recipes in the book, which meant over 30 victims. When I read Sophia's intro, the one that Harper had read out loud to me that last week in our home, something snapped in me.

I did that thing that all crazy, obsessed detectives did in movies: I made a crime wall. Pictures, lab reports, post it notes, colored string, the whole lot. I bought a world map at the dollar store in town. On it, I marked all the areas mentioned in the intros, as well as the description of the possible victims. She'd told me on the phone the night she fled that all the answers were there but hidden so no one could find them. But I would. I would find them all. Once I had everything organized, I started my investigation.

Since I started my pursuit of Harper, I've changed. I wasn't the clean-cut detective anymore. I had long hair now, graying at my temples, that I kept in a ponytail. I grew out my beard, too. I also dropped 40 pounds because I was too anxious or busy to eat. I was almost unrecognizable.

That was the first time I realized that Harper hadn't needed to try very hard to conceal her identity when she went on her killing spree. Something as simple as a ballcap or wearing your hair slightly differently was enough to camouflage a person completely.

The waitress came to my table, placed a small plate of bread pudding in front of me, and refilled my coffee cup. I took a bite of the bread pudding, and it was terrific. The hint of whiskey was just right: enough to be tasted but not so much as to overpower the rest of the ingredients. I moaned quietly, enjoying the small luxury.

When I was finished, the waitress returned to refill my coffee and take away the plate. "It's quite delicious, yeah? It's the *patissier's* signature dish."

"It was the best bread pudding I've ever had," I said. "Tell me, would there be any way for me to meet the chef? I have a few friends that work in the restaurant industry, and they've told me that chefs love hearing their food is appreciated. Does your chef have a minute?"

"I think Chef would quite love that, actually," she beamed. "We are between services now, so I think she can spare a moment. Let me check."

My back was to the kitchen door, but I heard it swing open. I heard the waitress talking to a woman with an Australian accent, but I didn't turn. The door swung open again as the chef came to my table. She sat down facing me. She was beautiful, even with the look of horror on her face.

"Hello, Harper," I said quietly.

She said nothing. Her eyes glanced around the café, deciding if she could escape without causing a scene. Her hair was long now, cascading down her shoulders in bright red waves. She looked like she had gained some weight. She had more curves than angles on her body now. I would've been so happy to see her if I weren't so angry at her.

"Harper?" she questioned in the Australian accent. "I don't know who Harper is. My name is Hannah."

"That's what you're going by now, huh?"

"I don't know what you're talking about, sir, but I don't appreciate your tone." She stood up and pointed at the door. "I'd like you to leave."

"No," I replied.

"Sir, please don't make me call the guarda."

"I don't think that will be necessary," I said. "The police chief is right over there."

I pointed to a portly man sitting in the corner, who looked at us over his newspaper. Then to two women sitting beside the door. "And those are two Interpol agents. And those," I nodded at three men, "Are MI5 and MI6. There are a few other agencies here as well, and officers covering the front and the back doors."

Her face dropped, and she began stuttering. I held a hand up to stop her. "Sit, Harper."

She obeyed, plopping hard into a chair and folding her arms tightly over her chest.

"How did you find me?" she grumbled, dropping the Australian accent.

"Your cookbook, in fact," I said. I reached into my bag and pulled out the copy Harper sent me all those years ago. Slips of paper stuck out the top of the book, noting all the details that correlated with evidence.

"Let's start with Francois, the *patissier* from Paris. You said he had a boring American name to throw off that his name literally means *France*. You also mentioned a fire. Imagine my surprise when I came across a report of a pastry chef killed when his *patisserie* burned with him inside. His assistant and shop keeper were unharmed, but no one ever heard from his trainee again."

She glared at me. "Sounds like a stretch."

"I would agree, except I contacted the detective on that case. He was able to get a copy of your visa paperwork. You lied about some details, but the important things matched."

She didn't speak, just clinched her jaw in anger.

"Then there's Tobias, the old man from Greece that you called Kostos. Your last outing with him was to scuba dive in a cave. I found a newspaper article about the death of an elderly diver who they suspected had his gear tampered with. He also happened to own a bunch of restaurants.

"Then I investigated Polish tourist trains. I wasn't surprised to find an unsolved case involving a young woman's body was found alongside the tracks. Her injuries were consistent with being thrown from a train. Her family owned a bagel company.

"The Australian one, though, was probably your best. I haven't been able to find any concrete evidence. A young Aboriginal woman was reported missing around the time you were there. She was supposedly hosting an American before she disappeared. You mentioned in the intro being afraid of all the dangerous animals in Australia. I'm guessing you murdered her and then took her body out where the wild animals would get it before anyone could find it."

"Those all sound like you pulled them from a crappy cop show," she said.

I ignored her. "You were the one that committed the crimes; I just followed the clues."

"You can't prove I had anything to do with any of those deaths," she spat. "Those could all have been accidents, and you don't have any evidence to the contrary. Even having proof that I was in that country during the murders isn't enough to get a conviction."

"I think you're wrong. All of these people," I motioned to the room, "Have been very invested in helping me establish a timeline of your whereabouts and suspicious deaths. They've been looking into recent murders, as well. Starting when I found you two years ago in Tokyo, just so you know."

Her eyes grew large, but she said nothing.

"I got to thinking to myself, how are you supporting yourself? You changed your identity, so I couldn't track you by Harper Cassidy. But I knew you couldn't stay out of the kitchen. And you couldn't access our joint accounts without leading the police directly to you.

"That's when I remembered all the time and energy you put into your cookbook. There was no way you wouldn't reap the rewards of all your hard work. The book was a hit, too, even more so after the news broke about you being a suspect in four murders. People couldn't buy your cookbook fast enough.

"The money from your sales wasn't going into our joint account. I contacted your publisher and got a subpoena for your financial records. I called in a few favors from my cybersecurity friends, and they were able to track the payments to an offshore account in the Cayman Islands. Once I had the account information, it wasn't hard to follow it around the world.

"You had been in Tokyo for almost a year by the time I tracked you down. Fortunately for you, getting an extradition warrant and coordinating everything with Japanese officials took long enough for you to move on. The same thing happened again eight months later in Nepal. Then a year ago in Rio. After four years, though, I had contacts in almost every country. And they were all ready and eager to bring you in. I've got a long list of countries that have unexplained disappearances and murders that they would like to talk to you about."

"Not that it'll do them any good," Harper mumbled.

I ignored her. "It was by a little bit of luck that we caught you here in Ireland, but we had everything in place to catch you before you could leave."

"What tipped you off?"

"It wasn't a murder. It was your cooking. I found an article about an Australian chef that had opened a café in Dingle. I checked your accounts, and, sure enough, you rented an AirBnB for six months. We all came to get you before you could kill anyone else."

"I haven't killed anyone, I assure you," she said. "So, there's nothing else for you to do here, Dawson."

"Unfortunately, that's not right, either." I stood up and reached into my pocket, removing a pair of handcuffs. "Harper Cassidy, you are under arrest for the murders of Grace Whitmore, Callum McIntyre, Ling Chan…and Sophia Leoni. You have the right—"

Outside the café, I watched the Chief of Police put Harper in the backseat of a police car. She looked straight ahead as she was taken to jail. There were half a dozen agents from different bureaus around the world that were keeping an eye on her. She wouldn't slip away this time. She would be questioned by the agents here in Ireland, then extradited to the United States, where we could prove she was guilty. As other countries built their cases against her, she would also have to answer to them.

"Detective, would you like a ride back to the station?" a Guarda officer asked.

"No, officer, I'm headed back to Dublin. I've got a plane to catch. There's a US Marshall at the station that will escort Mrs. Cassidy back to the United States."

Two days later, I was in Graceland Cemetery in Chicago.

"I got her, Sophia," I said to the marble stone.

The headstone read, "Sophia Graziella Leoni. Born September 15th, 1992, Died August 26th, 2022. Decorated Detective Killed in the Line of Duty." Beside her was her father's stone and then her grandmother's. She was back home.

"We found her in Ireland. It took four years, but she'll be brought back in the next few days for her arraignment. She won't get bail since she's an obvious flight risk. Soon, she'll be behind bars where she belongs. I've already contacted Grace, Callum, and Ling's families. They are happy to finally be able to put this behind them. I am, too, to be honest."

The wind blew through the trees in the cemetery. Orange and red leaves fell onto the ground and were swept away. The air smelled fresh, and only the faintest murmur of city traffic could be heard.

"This is a beautiful place," I said. "Far prettier than you ever let on. It's too bad I waited so long to come here. I should've visited you sooner, but it's been hard. I've felt a lot of guilt over what happened to you.

"I know, I know. Quit feeling sorry for myself, right? You knew this was a possibility when you joined the force. And would I be as upset if you were a man? I would answer 'yes' because I'm not one of those stoney cops in the movies we hate. But you're right; it's time to move on. I miss you, but it's time to start a new adventure in my life."

I set my hand on her headstone. "I know exactly what I'm going to do," I told her. "I'm going to go get some deep-dish pizza."

www.ingramcontent.com/pod-product-compliance
Lightning Source LLC
Chambersburg PA
CBHW072251270326
41930CB00010B/2342